Self-Help Groups and Human Service Agencies: How They Work Together

Daniel Remine, Robert M. Rice, and Jenny Ross

Family Service America   New York

Library of Congress Cataloging in Publication Data

Remine, Daniel, 1945–
   Self-help groups and human service agencies.

   Bibliography: p.
   1. Self-help groups--United States--Case studies.
2. Social service--United States--Case studies.
3. Family Service America. I. Rice, Robert M.,
1930-   . II. Ross, Jenny, 1955-   . III. Family
Service America. IV. Title.
HV547.R45 1984   362.8'2   83-48645
ISBN 0-87304-204-2

CONTENTS

Introduction 5

1. Self-Help Groups: When and Why 9
   Definitions and Characteristics

2. Self-Help Groups and Formal Service
   Providers 16
   Benefits of Cooperation

3. The Survey Process 24
   Representativeness of Sample

4. The Survey Findings. 29
   Agency Size...Contacts with Groups...
   Self-Help Group Concerns...Working with
   Groups...Current Relationships...Origin
   of Groups...Problems-Services Ratio...
   How Much of a Burden?...Discontinuing
   Contact

5. In-Depth Interviews. 71
   The Decision About Involvement...Types
   of Professional Assistance...Advantages
   of Relationships...Disadvantages...In-
   Put from Groups

6. Implications 83
   Factors Influencing Involvement...Lack
   of Medium Level Services...Absence of
   Interchange...Cycles of Self-Help
   Groups...The Need for Standards...The
   Need for Process...Reasons for Optimism

Appendix 97

Bibliography 105

INTRODUCTION

This book offers to all persons and organizations who may be interested in its subject the results of a survey carried on in 1982-83 by Family Service America (FSA), which at that time was known as Family Service Association of America.

FSA's interest in self-help groups stems from both local and national sources. On the local level, throughout the 1970s, the organization's member agencies observed the growth of self-help groups and began to relate to them in a variety of ways. The groups and the agencies served some of the same target populations. They shared many goals concerned with preventing or alleviating family and personal problems, although they sought to achieve these goals through different strategies and philosophies.

Many self-help groups had their roots in family service agencies. They may have been spin-offs from agency programs, independently initiated by agency staff, or planned as an adjunct to agency programs. Most agencies offer programs for groups with relatively loose structure and participant defined agendas. Family life education created an environment favorable to the creation of self-help groups. Participants would continue their contact and mutual support beyond the time limits of the programs.

Agency workers started groups on their own. Their impetus may have been to provide service beyond agency parameters or to supplement agency efforts. The agencies for whom they worked generally were accepting of these activities.

Family service agencies themselves have initiated self-help groups, deciding, for example, that certain target populations could best be reached and served through such groups. They may have been asked by their communities to sponsor groups such as Parents Anonymous. Occasionally, funding opportunities gave agencies an extra incentive for founding groups.

The agencies also were developing ties with independently formed groups, the incentive coming from either side. Agencies could reach out to the groups as community resources which could broaden their services and clientele. Self-help groups might see family agencies as offering needed space, administrative aid, endorsement, and referrals.

While the agencies developed a variety of relationships with the groups, the ties were informal and ad hoc. Agencies did not, as a rule, formulate organizational or program policies clarifying the place of self-help groups. They had not explored the variety of intermediary functions that they could perform.

On the national level, both experience and environment heightened FSA's interest in the groups. In the 1960s, it was involved in Project ENABLE with the National Urban League and the Child Study Association. Fifty-nine member agencies served as demonstration sites, combining family life education and community organization in outreach to poor and isolated populations. The groups that were organized frequently developed lives of their own and became effective mutual support groups.

In 1979, John McKnight, Associate Director of Northwestern University's Center for Urban Affairs, was well received when he addressed the FSA National Biennial Conference on the need for family service professionals to be helpful to self-help groups.

The 1980 White House Conference on Families and Children, in which both national and local levels of family service were deeply involved, emphasized its interest in self help and self help's potential for preventing family problems.

At the 1980 Wingspread Conference on Social Change and Family Services, agency executives expressed interest in aiding self-help groups. While they reported much activity with such groups, there was little conceptualization of the activity or integration of it in their program formats. The conference report recognized the need for family service agencies to incorporate "the challenge of promoting healthy self-help activities" in planning for the 80s.

The New World Foundation issued a 1980 report entitled Initiatives for Community Self-Help: Efforts to Increase Recognition and Support. It outlined a variety of action strategies for intermediary organizations, most of which FSA found particularly applicable to its member agencies. FSA felt, however, that it needed more complete and structured information on the quality and quantity of relationships between the agencies and self-help groups. Thus it undertook the study reported here.

The results of the study should be pertinent to the interests and activities of many kinds of organizations in the human service field, whether they are agencies with established programs --

referred to here as formal service providers -- or self-help groups on both the local and national levels. To encourage readers to appropriate the report for their own concerns, our text refers to FSA and family service only when clarity and accuracy seem to demand it. It speaks usually of "the national organization" rather than FSA, "agencies" rather than family service agencies, and "groups" rather than self-help groups.

1

SELF-HELP GROUPS: WHEN AND WHY

Self-help groups have had a long and varied history. Katz and Bender trace them back to the eighteenth century English friendly societies, which were trade organizations that established standards for work and pay and provided support for members who became ill. In nineteenth century England and America, consumer cooperatives, trade unions, immigrant aid societies and worker housing, banking, and educational programs had elements of self help.

The focus of self help in the twentieth century became less economic and more personal. Hurvitz stresses the religious and secular roots of their personal emphasis. The religious tradition was first programmed in Alcoholics Anonymous, with its emphasis on guilt, estrangement from the group, repentance, and reunion. Groups in this tradition foster confession, inspirational activities, and a historical, insight-oriented approach. The secular tradition, initially expressed in Recovery Inc., emphasizes will and responsibility. Secular groups focus on learning theory and a here-and-now approach.

Dumont adds that self-help groups are in the American philosophical mainstream. They are empirical and pragmatic: "Truth is what works and no value system is externally valid."

The last fifteen years have brought a dramatic increase in the number and variety of self-help groups. Gartner and Riessman report more than half a million such groups. They exist for nearly every major disease, age group, problem, and life situation.

Katz and Bender note two explanatory factors in the recent increase in self-help groups -- consumerism and professional acknowledgement. In describing the former they stress consumer frustration at the failure of established programs to provide services to certain groups and for certain problems. It might be added that the present generation of people in need are more likely to be educated and to feel that they have the power to develop alternative systems. Katz and Bender note that in both theory and practice, social services admit that it is necessary to involve clients in decisions about their treatment.

Silverman offers further insight into the increase in self-help groups. She believes that some groups form in response to professional failures. Their members may see traditional casework methods as ineffectual in dealing with their problems. They may want the less structured, more personal atmosphere offered by a self-help group.

Self-help groups frequently are organized around a chronic condition (alcoholism or child abuse, for example) that affects members' lives. These groups promote a pattern of conduct and provide some control over members' behavior. Other groups develop in reaction to new medical technology. Progress in medical and psychiatric treatment allows individuals who previously would have died or been institutionalized to continue constructive lives. However, since their medical and psychiatric problems frequently are not so much solved as in remission, they often coalesce for social and emotional support. Such groups focus on living with illness and support research and education.

Some groups are generated by the effect of social change on normal life transitions. In such areas of birth, child rearing, divorce, and death, societal standards and customs are becoming more varied. Individuals going through these transitions may not have familial and community resources to offer support and advice. Self-help groups form in response to these needs; the groups not only help members but also heighten societal awareness.

Definitions and Characteristics

According to Katz and Bender, self-help groups are small groups structured for mutual aid in the accomplishment of a specific purpose. They are usually formed by people who have come together for mutual assistance in satisfying a common need, overcoming a common handicap or life-disrupting problem, or bringing about a desired personal or social change. The initiators and members of such groups perceive that their needs are not or cannot be met through existing social institutions. To this description Gartner and Riessman add features that they feel are critical to self-help groups. These include face-to-face interactions, spontaneous origins, personal participation, agreed upon and engaged actions, and initial conditions of powerlessness. They also see such a group as a reference point, base for activity, and source of ego reinforcement.

Spiegel is more optimistic about the role of professionals and formal institutions in meeting the needs of people. He says that self-help and support groups are voluntary associations of individuals with a common problem, stigma, or life situation; the associations involve no professional control, although there may be professional activity of a consultative type. He adds that such groups make no financial profit. They usually engage in a combination of mutual aid to members and to the public and in political activity.

Tracy and Gussow divide health focused self-help associations into what they call Type I and Type II groups. Type I groups provide direct assistance such as education, coping skills, and group support to patients and relatives. Examples include Alcoholics Anonymous and Overeaters Anonymous. Type II groups focus on the whole population of individuals afflicted with a particular medical problem. Activities include the promotion of research, fund raising, public education, and lobbying. Examples are the National Heart Association and the American Diabetic Association.

This perspective is related to Katz and Bender's labeling groups by their degree of inner or outer focus. Inner focused groups are centered on their members and devoted to their immediate constituency. In contrast, outer focused groups stress societal goals such as welfare reform and acceptance of alternate lifestyles. Of course the division is not absolute. Type I or inner groups occasionally perform Type II tasks. Because of the scope of their goals, Type II or outer groups are likely to become more structured and to assume many of the characteristics of formal service providers -- established service organizations with specific programs. Family service agencies frequently have programs that are community oriented. However, their primary focus is on the problems of families and individuals. They are more likely to relate to similarly focused Type I groups.

Self-help groups by definition deal with problems. The social acceptability of a group's problem area is another way of classifying it. Society is likely to accept groups whose problem -- a medical condition or widowhood, for example -- it sees as beyond the control of the sufferer. Smoking or overeating represent another type of problem, one that is seen as the responsibility of the individual but is generally tolerated. A third problem type -- alcoholism and gambling are examples -- is not socially acceptable and is seen as the fault of the individual. Child abuse is typical of the fourth type -- socially stigmatic with blame placed on the individual.

Self-help groups can be ordered by their association with other organizations. They may be affiliated to national or regional self-help groups. Such organizations may offer structure and guidance to new groups and relate them to a broader focus. A group may start independently. It is possible that the problem on which the group focuses is in some way unique. The group simply may not want to affiliate with a larger organization. Finally, groups may be initiated by or at least related to formal service providers.

The classification of self-help groups most relevant to the purposes of this report probably is Leon Levy's four-part typology based on purpose and composition. His Type I groups emphasize conduct reorganization or behavioral control. Alcoholics Anonymous, Take Off Pounds Sensibly, and Parents Anonymous are among groups representative of this type. Type II groups are those whose members share a predicament which entails a degree of stress. Their aim is not to change the situation but to ameliorate the stress. Examples include Parents Without Partners and Make Today Count. Type III groups are survival-oriented, with members that society has discriminated against or labeled deviant. The groups' aims include both mutual support and consciousness raising to enhance self-esteem and publicity and political activity aimed at societal acceptance and elimination of discrimination. Black pride and gay groups would fall in this category. Members of Type IV groups share goals of personal growth, self-actualization, and enhanced effectiveness in life. There is no central, shared concern but members bring problems to such a group in the belief that together members can help each other to better lives. A sensitivity group is an example of such a group.

Leon Levy lists nine helping activities that are offered by self-help groups: empathy, mutual affirmation, explanation, sharing, morale building, self-disclosure, positive reenforcement, personal goal setting, and catharsis. Leonard Borman notes five curative factors that are found in self-help groups: (1) universality, or recognition by group members that they are not alone in their problems; (2) acceptance of the problem rather than disapproval; (3) hope that the problem can be dealt with; (4) altruism or self-esteem through the experience of giving help; and (5) cognitive restructuring, which may involve a detailed belief system or simply new knowledge about the cause and effect of problems.

The literature on self-help groups is for the most part positive about them. Yet the groups do have their limitations. Milofsky notes that "voluntaristic organizations are hard to establish and maintain. They demand great energy on the part of leaders and are vulnerable to moderate changes in their environment." By their nature they are fluid and transient. Members -- and more importantly, leaders -- frequently change as their problems are resolved and they lose interest. Some leaders assume too much responsibility and burn out. There is no self-sustaining structure to assure continuity.

Internal problems of the groups may result in conflict or exclusiveness. Unresolved problems, regarding leadership or focus, for example, may cause their dissolution. Looking inward for support, groups may become closed, dependent on core members, and no longer open to others who need help.

The groups serve only a partial function in the resolution of problems. Alcoholics Anonymous, as an example, may help an alcoholic maintain sobriety but it does not claim to resolve deep seated issues which therapy might probe.

Finally, in attempting to solve problems, self-help groups have both quantitative and qualitative limitations. In the former instance, a focus on one problem may mean a lack of insight on inter-relatedness with other problems. In some situations, the individual's problem on which a self-help group is working may deepen and require professional help. Whether the group can or will make a referral for such help is problematic.

2

SELF-HELP GROUPS AND FORMAL SERVICE PROVIDERS

While self-help groups and agencies that are formal service providers share clientele and services, the relationship between them has not been without stress. The stress comes both from the history of self-help groups and the inherent natures of the two types of organizations.

As we have noted, many of the groups were founded because of dissatisfaction with the services of agencies. The groups often pioneered services in areas such as child abuse and response to illness that agencies had not considered part of their mandate. The groups often regarded the agencies with hostility or considered them irrelevant to their purposes. Further, many groups were founded during the 1960s and 70s when society in general and social science literature in particular were suspicious of agencies and doubted that self-help groups could work with them without being co-opted.

Milofsky notes that groups are more personal and less systematic than agencies. Group members offer help to one another at no or low cost. Identification between members is encouraged. Meetings are held in diverse settings; groups have relatively little bureaucratic structure; there is a minimum of such complexities as a chain of command, records, and appointments. In contrast, agencies use professional, authoritative staff to provide services for fees. Clients' identification with workers generally is discouraged. Agencies usually offer help in formal office settings and have full bureaucratic frameworks.

Groups' linkages with agencies that are formal caregivers frequently are ad hoc. The fluidity of group structures may cause problems in maintaining these linkages. Agencies have definite boundaries; they try to develop interagency linkages which are routine and economical.

The hierarchical structure of formal service agencies, while it may negate spontaneity and flexibility, does allow for planning and decision making. As organizations, self-help groups are more oriented to the present than the future. Their leadership, if it changes frequently, may pose problems in establishing a center of responsibility.

The historic atmosphere of suspicion and the basic differences between groups and agencies have been reflected in a variety of interorganizational problems. The key problem is one of autonomy. Milofsky notes that a major dilemma of self-help groups is maintaining independence -- insuring that they are not taken over when interacting with more powerful organizations. Groups may see advantages in the administratively neat structures of formal service agencies, but need to be wary of becoming too dependent on such structures. The loss of a group's independence may be disadvantageous to a related agency as well; it may want to preserve the flexibility and personal support of the self-help group. Agencies do not want the administrative and financial responsibility that a co-opted self-help group may entail.

The "fit" of a group-agency relationship is another problem, especially for the agency. Does

the focus of a group fall within the parameters of
the agency's mission? Will the relationship be
accepted by the larger community of which the agency is a part? Can the agency really contribute
anything to the group?

Reliability in terms of service and continuity
is a concern for both parties. An agency may be
reluctant to refer clients to a group which does
not have systems for quality assurance, case planning, or record keeping. A self-help group may not
want to share clients with an organization that
provides what they perceive as impersonal and im-
practical services. Groups may be perceived by
formal service agencies as organizations suscepti-
ble to rapid change and demise. An agency may not
be eager to develop ties with what it sees as a
temporary group.

Finally, while both agencies and groups may see
the need for cooperation, in practice they may be
threatened by it. Collaboration necessitates the
acceptance of a variety of formal and informal ways
of helping people. It may engender feelings of
defensiveness, inadequacy, and resentment from both
professionals and group members.

Benefits of Cooperation

Fortunately, the incentives for cooperation
between groups and agencies outweigh the disincen-
tives. In her discussion of the relation between
community mental health services and mutual assistance groups, Chutis notes that agencies and groups
share broadly based goals and target populations.
Both types of organizations generally strive to
increase the ability of individuals to cope and to
decrease social and psychological disabilities.
They both offer services to prevent problems or
reduce their severity. Each tries to reach underserved populations. The services of groups and
agencies are supportive and educational in nature.

Collaborative efforts involving groups and agencies can be advantageous to both types of organizations and to their clients. Groups may benefit from the specialized knowledge and skills of agency professionals. Through association with agencies they may gain greater legitimacy, acceptance, and access to community funding and power sources.

In certain situations, for example, those involving social stigma or loss of support systems, agency professionals may see self-help groups as sources of the most effective treatment. Groups may provide consumer input to agencies and they also may develop political support for agency programs.

The cooperation of agencies and groups increases the amount and variety of help that can be offered to clients. With this broader scope, individual service plans can be made more complete. More people can be reached.

In its 1980 report, Initiatives for Community Self Help: Efforts to Increase Recognition and Support, The New World Foundation created a comprehensive listing of the various types of organizations that could aid self-help groups and the concrete services the organizations could offer. It included formal service providers.

On a broader level, according to Biegel and Naparstek, government has expressed a growing interest in self-help groups as a way to maximize social service delivery. The government sees self-help groups as a way to reach underserved people, as demonstrated by the 1978 report of the President's Commission on Mental Health. Self-help groups often attract those individuals and groups unlikely to reach out for traditional therapeutic help from agencies.

Professionals already are positively involved with self-help groups. Spiegel's review of the literature concludes that despite potential problems, professionals have a positive relationship with the groups. Many of the original groups such as Recovery Inc. were started by professionals; others such as Parents Anonymous depend upon formal service providers as sponsors and professional staff as co-leaders to help them guide meetings, according to Borkman and Chutis. A survey by Steinman and Traunstein showed that many professionals had initiated groups or had been members themselves. Todres notes that social work professionals are more aware of a larger number of self-help groups than are doctors, nurses, psychiatrists, or psychologists.

Finally, there are indications that self-help groups can work positively with agencies without being co-opted. Borman discusses ten self-help groups founded or supported by agencies which have continued to exist independently.

How can formal service agencies and self-help groups develop constructive collaborative efforts? Gottlieb suggests that each type of organization begin by recognizing the valuable and unique contribution of the other. Silverman notes that "the organizational setting in which the work is carried out and the (self) helper's relation to that organization affects the nature of the help offered." She feels that the established agency should state explicitly the limit of its relationship with the self-help group, allowing the group to evolve naturally. Chutis outlines four principles for mental health professionals working with such groups: (1) power and authority lie within the group, not the professional; (2) emphasis should be placed on the group's behavior, skills, and problem solving rather than intrapsychic dynamics; (3) the group's

strengths rather than weaknesses should be emphasized; (4) in work with the groups, the diagnostic
ability of the professional is not as important as
her or his skills in community organization, group
work, and communication.

Agencies may engage themselves with self-help
groups in a variety of intermediary roles according
to the literature. There are three broad categories based on the degree of interaction and commitment required of both organizations.

On the most removed level, agencies may refer
clients to groups. Chutis says that referrals may
be reciprocated as groups send clients in need of
therapeutic intervention to professional agencies.
Referral necessitates mutual knowledge of services
and resources on the part of both agencies and
groups. By itself, it probably does not constitute
an endorsement.

On a level of closer contact, the roles of an
agency may include that of liaison between a group
and the formal service community. The New World
Foundation notes that this function may include the
creation of mechanisms for regular agency-group
interaction, including planning and resource allo-
cation. Liaison is not an easy role, and the
formal provider that assumes it may have to deal
with the suspicion of both types of organizations.

Formal providers may develop self-help clearing-
houses or directories with or without endorsing
groups. Lieberman and Borman note that a clearinghouse might advertise, promote, and support self-
help organizations, thus serving the groups,
professionals, and the community at large. Agencies also can recruit for the groups.

Regular training and technical assistance can be
provided by an agency. Its staff, serving as guest

speakers at self-help group meetings, can provide information of interest and relevance. Borman reports that three-fourths of the mutual aid groups he surveyed indicated this kind of contact. Training frequently centers on group leaders. Silverman suggests that professionals see training as helping volunteers appreciate their own knowledge and experience. Role playing and discussion rather than formal lectures should be emphasized.

Most self-help groups operate on a minimal budget. Chutis feels that agencies can offer needed support services such as fund raising, clerical assistance, supplies, meeting space, and publicity. They also can assist with research and information that will help groups carry out their activities.

The New World Foundation notes the need for organizations to serve as funding buffers for self-help groups -- accepting wholesale grants and retailing them to a variety of groups.

Agencies can help groups with consultation (frequently on a time limited basis) regarding group process, leadership, evaluation, and individual cases. Agency staff may serve on group advisory boards. They may staff or co-lead a group. As previously noted, Parents Anonymous invites professional organizations to sponsor and provide skills to local groups -- but not to set policy for them. Chutis says that in these situations two rules should be stressed to maintain group autonomy: a self-help member should be chairperson for the group and the professional staff person should be a volunteer not paid by his or her agency for providing service. The sponsoring agency also may be a buffer against possible community hostility.

An agency may either sponsor a local chapter of a national self-help group or create a new local group. This activity is the most complicated level of involvement. Chutis delineates how agencies can establish priorities, identify high risk populations, develop task forces, and outline the boundaries of groups that they form. Agencies have the potential to help such groups get off the ground with the goal of becoming autonomous, according to Froland. However, the timing and degree of autonomy must be worked out on an individual case basis.

3

THE SURVEY PROCESS

The relationships between self-help groups and formal service agencies that are described with a broad brush in the preceding chapter have been demonstrated in the specific experiences with such groups reported by agencies that are members of Family Service America (FSA). When The New World Foundation issued its report in 1980 on ways to increase support of self-help groups, FSA, from the perspective of nearly twenty years of experience, found many points of affirmation.

Analyzing this experience convinced the organization that future involvement with self-help groups would be best developed if it was based on detailed information. Thus FSA undertook a survey of its member agencies in 1982-83 to obtain data on four different levels.

On a concrete level, it required knowledge of how many member agencies had any relations with self-help groups and how many and what kinds of groups were involved. Whether such contacts had increased or decreased also was important.

On a process level, the organization wanted insight into how relationships were established, the decision-making process behind them, and the roles played by local agencies. It wanted to know about the advantages and the problems of relationships between agencies and groups. It also sought information about the effect of community attitudes -- supportive or discouraging -- on such relationships.

On a philosophical level, FSA wanted to learn whether member agencies or self-help groups had philosophies to guide them in interrelating, and what was their effect.

The broadest focus of interest was on potential development. The organization was looking for feedback on the possibility of more local contacts with self-help groups and the various levels at which such contacts could develop. Such information might result in an effort to recruit agencies in a cooperative venture focused on relations with the groups. The national organization needed to know if its agencies wanted guidelines or a program modality to maximize their work with the groups.

To provide the substantial amount of information that would be required to meet these needs, the organization developed a two-part questionnaire. A copy of it appears in the appendix. The first part explored the overall relationship of agencies to self-help groups; the second asked for information on agency relationships with specific self-help groups. The memo accompanying the questionnaire gave a definition of self-help groups as "primary groups which are directed to personal or social concerns and which depend primarily on their own members' participation to control and implement their program." It asked respondents to utilize that definition in their answers.

Section I of the instrument began by questioning member agencies about their involvement with self-help groups. Levels of involvement included provision of information on, referrals to, and services for self-help groups. Member agencies were asked

about changes in their involvement with self-help
groups and about factors (such as agency policy,
finances, and national organization guidance) that
might influence such change. Finally, agencies
were asked whether FSA should provide information
and other assistance to help them in their relations with self-help groups; specific reasons for
their answers were requested.

Member agencies were requested to complete a
separate copy of Section II of the questionnaire
for each self-help group with which they had an
individual relationship.

Section II sought information about the size and
service population of each self-help group to which
agencies were related. It also focused on each
group's overall missions and specific objectives.
Agencies were queried as to the auspices of self-
help groups with which they cooperated. They were
asked about their role regarding leadership, training, finances, administration, and connections with
other groups. A variety of potential problems in
the relationships -- for example, control, ideology, and cohesion -- were explored. Finally, the
status of each arrangement -- continuing or terminated (with reason for termination) -- was covered.
Agencies were asked about their roles regarding
leadership, training, finances, administration, and
making connections with other groups.

On January 25, 1982, the questionnaire was
mailed to 260 member agencies. By the survey dead-
line thirteen months later, 154 responses had been
received -- a response rate of fifty-nine percent.

Another phase of the survey, planned to supplement the use of the questionnaire, was instituted
in early 1983. The national organization sent a
staff member to a representative sample of the
agencies that had responded to the questionnaire.

Her assignment was to interview the staff of the
agencies and members of self-help groups with which
the agencies were associated. The purpose of the
interviews was to obtain more detailed information
than questionnaire answers provided about relationships between agencies and groups. A full report
of these interviews appears in chapter five.

Representativeness of Sample

To verify the representativeness of the respondents to the questionnaire, the survey team compared agencies replying to the questionnaire to
those not responding. Comparisons were made in
regard to such characteristics as size, sponsorship, budget, location, clientele, and other
affiliations. The process showed that, over all,
agencies responding to the questionnaire were
representative of the national organization's membership.

However, the survey team still was interested in
whether agencies responding and those not responding were in any way different in the extent of
their involvement with self-help groups. Twelve
nonrespondents with characteristics similar to
respondent agencies in terms of size, location, and
sponsorship were identified. They were telephoned
and an abbreviated version of the questionnaire was
administered to their executives. Of the twelve,
ten had or presently were cooperating with at least
one group. None of the ten had generated groups of
their own but all referred clients to local chap-
ters of such groups as Parents Without Partners or
Alcoholics Anonymous. Staff members of a number of
the agencies had served on self-help group boards
or committees. All twelve agencies wanted FSA to
develop guidelines for communications and relationships with self-help groups.

This subsample has lead FSA to assume that agencies not responding to the questionnaire have only

a limited involvement with self-help groups but that most of them are aware of such groups and do refer to them.

4

THE SURVEY FINDINGS

The first set of questions covered the overall involvement of the national organization's member agencies with self-help groups (Table 1). One hundred and thirty-nine respondents (93 percent)* made referrals to self-help groups and one hundred and twenty-eight (85 percent) provided information on such groups to the community. Sixty-seven agencies (46 percent) encouraged self-help groups to connect with each other -- forty-seven to exchange services, sixty to exchange information, and forty-two for advocacy. Fifty-three (36 percent) agencies offered common services to several self-help groups, including information on community and agency resources (fifty-three respondents), information about personal relationships (forty respondents), and training in organization and administration of groups (twenty-nine respondents).

When asked about changes in the amount of their contacts with self-help groups, fifty-nine (49 percent) agencies noted an increase, fifty-five (46 percent) saw no change, and six (5 percent) reported decline. One hundred and two (77 percent) agencies wanted to expand their work with self-help groups while thirty (23 percent) did not. Ninety-nine of the agencies wanting to expand expressed

---

*All percentages are based on the number of respondents answering the question.

TABLE 1
AGENCIES' GENERAL SERVICES TO SELF-HELP GROUPS

		SERVICE PROVIDED				
		YES		NO		TOTAL	
SERVICE		NUMBER	%	NUMBER	%	NUMBER	%
I. Referrals to Self-Help Groups	139	(93)	11	(7)	150	(100)
II. Information on Self-Help Groups	128	(85)	23	(15)	151	(100)
III. Connections Between Self-Help Groups	67	(46)	80	(54)	147	(100)
A. To exchange services	47	(67)	23	(33)	70	(100)
B. To join forces for advocacy	42	(60)	28	(40)	70	(100)
C. To exchange information	60	(86)	10	(14)	70	(100)
D. Other	15*	–	–	–	–	–
IV. Common Services to Self-Help Groups	53	(36)	95	(64)	148	(100)
A. Leadership Training	28	(45)	34	(55)	62	(100)
B. Organizational/ Administrative Training	29	(46)	34	(54)	63	(100)
C. Information on Community/Agency Resources	53	(87)	8	(13)	61	(100)
D. Information About Personal Relationships	40	(67)	20	(33)	60	(100)
E. Other Services	27*	–	–	–	–	–

---

*"No" response was not possible in the "other services" categories.

willingness to work with the national organization
in a one-year cooperative activity focused on self-
help groups; thirty-nine of these said they would
cooperate whether or not they were paid for it.

Asked if the national organization should inform
and aid agencies in their work with self-help
groups, 104 (71 percent) agencies agreed, twenty-
nine (20 percent) were neutral, and thirteen (9
percent) disagreed. Of the 104 agencies in agreement, sixty-two (60 percent) thought that the
national organization should develop relations with
self-help groups into a modality with standards.
Sixty agencies (58 percent)* expected increased
involvement with self-help groups.

Agency Size
The researchers were interested in learning what
factors inherent in member agencies (size, affilia-
tion, population served) might influence the overall degree of their relations to self-help groups.
It was found that the most relevant factor was
agency staff size.

The types of involvement with self-help groups
mentioned in the first part of the questionnaire
(referral, connection with each other, offering
services to several groups in common) form a three-
part qualitative scale from least to most involvement. In Chart 1 these different levels of involvement are compared in agencies of different
sizes: small (one through ten staff members),
medium (eleven through thirty), and large (thirty-
one or more).

In each of the three types, the survey indicated
that large agencies are most likely to be involved
with self-help groups. Further, as involvement
deepens, especially in terms of offering services

---

*Duplicate answers to this question were possible.

CHART 1
STAFF SIZE AND LEVEL OF INVOLVEMENT WITH SELF-HELP GROUPS

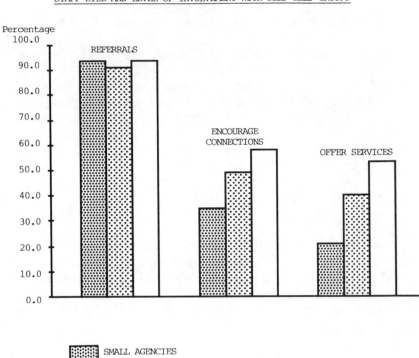

to several groups in common, the gap between large and small agencies widens. This pattern might be expected. Large agencies should have the potential resources to do more with self-help groups.

Cross tabulations also were completed on the size of responding agencies and the change in their work with self-help groups and desire to expand such work (Table 2). Large and especially medium size agencies were more likely to note growth in work with self-help groups and large agencies were most likely to note a desire to expand such contacts.

However, when asked if the national organization should provide information and help its agencies in other ways in their work with self-help groups, large agencies were most likely to respond negatively (25 percent), while small agencies (16 percent) were least likely. It may be that, with their experience and resources, large agencies are less likely to see how they could utilize national help in dealing with self-help groups. Small agencies -- short on experience and resources -- seem more amenable to aid.

Finally, it is significant that so many small agencies reported contact with self-help groups. Even with limited staff and time, they had established some relationship with these groups. They indicated their receptivity to aid and guidance in furthering these relationships.

Of the 154 respondents, 102 had at least one individualized relation with a self-help group and thus completed Section II of the questionnaire. In total, they had contact with 348 self-help groups -- more than the membership of most national self-help organizations.

TABLE 2
AGENCIES' STAFF SIZE AND EXPECTATION OF INVOLVEMENT WITH SELF-HELP GROUPS

	AGENCY STAFF SIZE					
	SMALL		MEDIUM		LARGE	
EXPECTATIONS	NUMBER	%	NUMBER	%	NUMBER	%
Involvement Increasing						
Yes	16	(33)	26	(65)	17	(53)
No	32	(67)	14	(35)	15	(47)
TOTAL	48	(100)	40	(100)	32	(100)
Wish to Expand Involvement						
Yes	42	(72)	33	(77)	27	(87)
No	16	(28)	10	(23)	4	(13)
TOTAL	58	(100)	43	(100)	31	(100)
National Organization Should Inform & Help Agencies in Relations with Self-Help Groups						
Positive Answers*	81	(75)	54	(72)	44	(70)
Neutral Answers	10	(9)	7	(9)	3	(5)
Negative Answers	17	(16)	14	(19)	16	(25)
TOTAL	108	(100)	75	(100)	63	(100)

*More than one answer possible per agency.

Contacts with Groups

The survey was interested in comparing local agencies without individualized relationships with self-help groups with those agencies which had such contacts. In Table 3 the two categories are shown by types of general involvement with self-help groups, desire to expand such involvement, and interest in national organization activities in the self-help area. Agencies without individual relationships were less likely to provide information on self-help groups or make referrals to them. They also were not as likely to wish to expand contact with such groups. They were more likely to be neutral regarding further national involvement with the self-help movement than agencies actively involved with such groups.

A number of agencies with no individual relations with self-help groups were polled as to why they had not developed such relationships. Several reported that they saw themselves as resources for groups but had not actually sought them out. Others said that some contact with the groups was made as part of their regular services or that they provided aid to such groups periodically but not consistently.

Returning to agencies with specific contacts with self-help groups: they related to from one to twenty groups. Thirty agencies focused on only one group, eighteen on two groups, twenty-nine on three or four groups, and twenty-three agencies on five or more groups.

It appears that agency size, as judged by number of staff members, is a determinant in the number of self-help groups with which agencies relate. Chart 2 portrays agency size and number of self-help groups served. As would be expected, large agencies are more likely to serve a relatively large number of self-help groups.

TABLE 3
INVOLVEMENT WITH SELF-HELP GROUPS AND DESIRE FOR NATIONAL ORGANIZATION
GUIDANCE IN THE MATTER OF WHETHER AGENCIES HAD INDIVIDUALIZED RELATIONSHIPS
WITH SELF-HELP GROUPS

	LEVEL OF RELATIONSHIP			
INVOLVEMENT/DESIRE	INDIVIDUALIZED		NOT INDIVIDUALIZED	
FOR GUIDANCE	NUMBER	(%)	NUMBER	(%)
Provide Information on Self Help Groups				
Yes	93	(93)	17	(34)
No	7	(7)	33	(66)
Refer to Self-Help Groups				
Yes	97	(99)	41	(80)
No	1	(1)	10	(20)
Wish to Expand Contact with Self-Help Groups				
Yes	74	(89)	27	(59)
No	9	(11)	19	(41)
Wish National Organization Involvement with Self-Help Groups				
Yes	126*	(75)	53	(68)
Neutral	9	(5)	11	(14)
No	33	(20)	14	(18)

*More than one answer possible per agency.

CHART 2
STAFF SIZE BY NUMBER OF SELF-HELP GROUPS WITH WHICH THEY RELATE

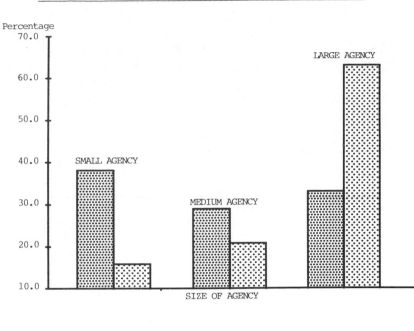

Percentage

LARGE AGENCY

SMALL AGENCY

MEDIUM AGENCY

SIZE OF AGENCY

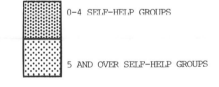

0-4 SELF-HELP GROUPS

5 AND OVER SELF-HELP GROUPS

Respondents identified seventy-seven self-help
groups (31 percent) as local, fourteen (6 percent)
as statewide, and 150 (62 percent) as national.
Five groups were classified as "other." Forty-one
groups (12 percent) primarily served a particular
ethnic group. Seventy-one groups (21 percent)
focused on particular income categories (forty-
eight on low and twenty-three on middle and high
income).

Self-Help Group Concerns

Using a list on the questionnaire, respondents
were given the chance to identify self-help groups
by the problem on which they concentrated. One
hundred and sixteen were so classified: sixty-three
focused on neglect and abuse, twenty-seven on the
elderly, eighteen on foster or institutional care,
and eight on developmentally disabled people.

The survey asked agencies about the objectives
of the self-help groups with which they had individual contact. There were four specific and an
"other" category. The first two categories --
individual member's problems and self improvement
-- would relate to Katz and Bender's "inner" focus,
while the other categories -- support of a way of
life and intervening for social change -- would
tend towards an "outer" focus. Groups were reported as having from one to five objectives, with 138
described as having one objective and ninety-four
as having two. The most common emphasis was the
problems of individual members; 288 groups (86
percent of the total) were focused on them. One
hundred and sixty-two groups (48 percent) stressed
self improvement while 114 (34 percent) supported a
way of life or philosophy. Intervention to change
social conditions was a reported objective of 104
groups (31 percent).

Many of the groups represented in the survey had

combinations of objectives. Table 4 indicates that
nearly one third of the groups (31 percent) were
concerned exclusively with individual problems; 7
percent stressed only self-improvement. Thirteen
percent had the combination of individual member's
problems and self-improvement as objectives. Thus,
all together, more than half of the groups func-
tioned exclusively within the most narrow problem
perspective. In contrast, the groups stressing
only a way of life, changing social conditions, or
the two in combination made up less than five
percent of the total.

When asked how the self-help groups with which
they interacted were organized, respondents reported that 104 (33 percent) were under agency auspices
while seventy-two (23 percent) were under the auspices of another organization and 143 (45 percent)
were independent.

Agencies were asked about the specific services
they offered to self-help groups. The questionnaire listed ten types of service and an "other"
category. Respondents reported from one to ten
types of involvement, with an average of 3.7 services offered.

In Chart 3 the ten specific services are ordered
into three groupings by degree of interaction and
communication. Low Interaction and Communication
indicates only referral of potential participants.
Medium Interaction and Communication includes
training or education; financing or help in finding
funds; administrative or physical support (meeting
space, clerical service, bookkeeping); connecting
groups with or informing them about community
resources beyond those in the agency; organizing
and recruiting activities; and research and information development to help a group carry out its
objectives. High Interaction and Communication
includes a group's primary leadership; professional

TABLE 4

SELF-HELP GROUP OBJECTIVES - SINGULARLY AND IN COMBINATION

OBJECTIVE	SELF-HELP GROUPS	
	NUMBER	(%)
Individual Member Problems	103	(31)
Self Improvement	23	(7)
Support Way of Life	6	(2)
Change Social Conditions	6	(2)
Individual Member's Problems and Self Improvement	43	(13)
Individual Member's Problems and Support Way of Life	15	(4)
Individual Member's Problems and Change Social Conditions	25	(7)
Self Improvement and Support Way of Life	6	(2)
Self Improvement and Change Social Conditions	3	(1)
Support Way of Life and Change Social Conditions	2	(--)*
Individual Members Problems, Self Improvement, and Support Way of Life	36	(11)
Individual Members Problems, Self Improvement, Change Social Conditions	19	(6)
Individual Members Problems, Support Way of Life, and Change Social Conditions	17	(5)
Self Improvement, Support Way of Life, Change Social Conditions	2	(--)*
Individual Members Problems, Self Improvement, Support Way of Life, and Change Social Conditions	30	(9)
TOTAL	336	(101)

---

*Less than one percent.

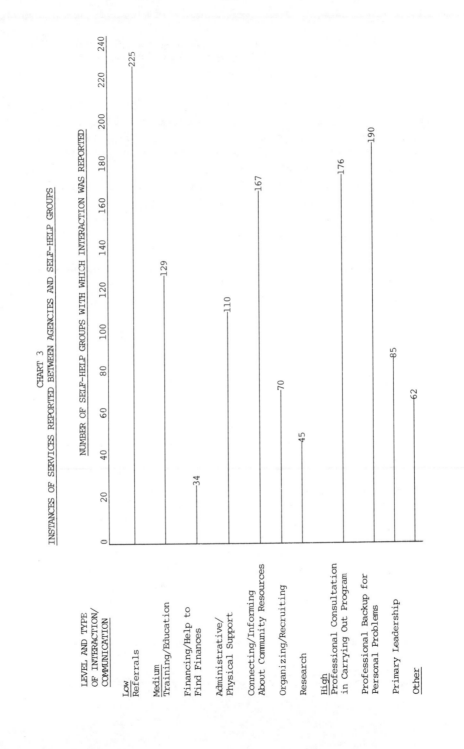

CHART 3

INSTANCES OF SERVICES REPORTED BETWEEN AGENCIES AND SELF-HELP GROUPS

NUMBER OF SELF-HELP GROUPS WITH WHICH INTERACTION WAS REPORTED

LEVEL AND TYPE
OF INTERACTION/
COMMUNICATION

Low
Referrals — 225

Medium
Training/Education — 129

Financing/Help to
Find Finances — 34

Administrative/
Physical Support — 110

Connecting/Informing
About Community Resources — 167

Organizing/Recruiting — 70

Research — 45

High
Professional Consultation
in Carrying Out Program — 176

Professional Backup for
Personal Problems — 190

Primary Leadership — 85

Other — 62

consultation in carrying out the basic program of a group as a whole; and professional backup to help with personal problems identified within the group.

The number of self-help groups for which each involvement were noted are listed in Chart 3. As might be expected, referrals in the Low Interaction and Communication category were most frequently reported. The next two most noted types of services -- professional consultation in carrying out the group's program and professional backup with personal problems -- fell into the High Interaction and Communication category. The fourth and fifth most reported services -- connecting/informing groups about other community resources and training/education -- are in the Medium Interaction and Communication grouping.

Overall, respondents offered 225 low level services, 555 medium level services and 451 high level services. The number of high level services, which involved the greatest commitment of resources, is impressive.

Chart 4 shows how the agencies provided the three levels of service singly and in combination to self-help groups. The agencies tended to offer services across the three levels. Over three-fourths of the self-help groups received service on more than one level and over two-fifths (41 percent) received some services on all three levels. Combining categories, 67 percent of self-help groups received at least one low interaction/communications service, 73 percent received at least one intermediate level interaction/communications service, and a surprisingly high 79 percent of self-help groups received at least one high interaction/communication level service.

Working with Groups
Agencies also were asked about problems they had

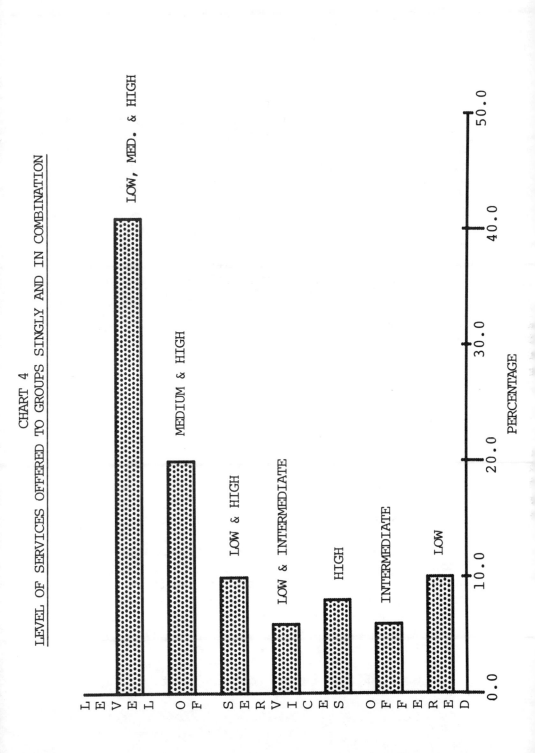

CHART 4

LEVEL OF SERVICES OFFERED TO GROUPS SINGLY AND IN COMBINATION

in working with self-help groups with which they had individualized relations. The questionnaire listed fourteen types of problems and an "other" category. One category, finances, was subdivided into (1) funding for work with the self-help group and (2) direct financing of the group. Responding agencies reported from zero to ten problems, with an average of 1.46 problems. Surprisingly, 135 (40 percent) of the agency-group relations involved no reported problems.

In Chart 5, the fourteen problems are ordered into three broad categories. The first of these encompasses problems that are inherent in the self-help group itself, problems that would exist even if the group had no relationship with the agency. This category includes: (1) too much or too little activity demanded of participants in group; (2) group activity inappropriate for most participants; (3) inadequate group leadership; (4) problems with the nature of participation by group members; and (5) difficulties with cohesion within the group.

The second category includes problems in the relationship between the agency and the group, especially in terms of power and communications. It includes: (1) problems with auspices and control; (2) competition between the group and the agency; (3) overdependence on the agency; (4) differences over ethics and ideology; and (5) lack of coordination between the agency and the group.

The third collection of problems focuses on how much support the agencies can offer self-help groups, including the availability of resources and community environment. It incorporates: (1) difficulties in recruiting for the group; (2) financing; (3) keeping the group alive; and (4) community hostility to the group's activities.

As Chart 5 shows, the most frequently mentioned

CHART 5
INSTANCES OF PROBLEMS REPORTED BETWEEN AGENCIES AND SELF-HELP GROUPS

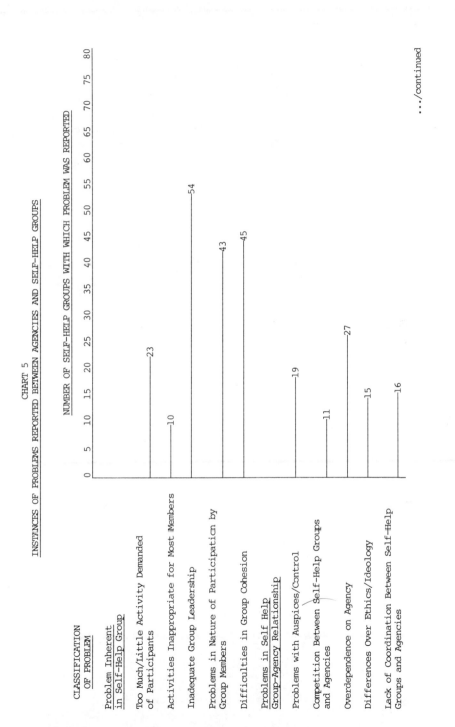

NUMBER OF SELF-HELP GROUPS WITH WHICH PROBLEM WAS REPORTED

CLASSIFICATION
OF PROBLEM

Problem Inherent
in Self-Help Group

Too Much/Little Activity Demanded
of Participants — 23

Activities Inappropriate for Most Members — 10

Inadequate Group Leadership — 54

Problems in Nature of Participation by
Group Members — 43

Difficulties in Group Cohesion — 45

Problems in Self Help
Group-Agency Relationship

Problems with Auspices/Control — 19

Competition Between Self-Help Groups
and Agencies — 11

Overdependence on Agency — 27

Differences Over Ethics/Ideology — 15

Lack of Coordination Between Self-Help
Groups and Agencies — 16

.../continued

46

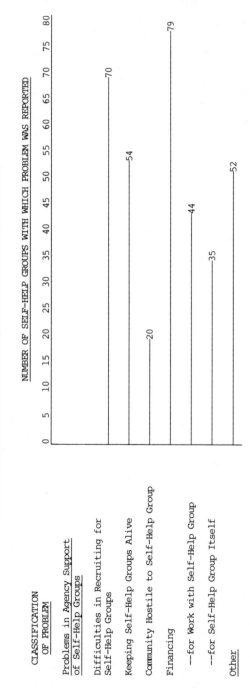

CHART 5 (Cont'd)

INSTANCES OF PROBLEMS REPORTED BETWEEN AGENCIES AND SELF-HELP GROUPS

NUMBER OF SELF-HELP GROUPS WITH WHICH PROBLEM WAS REPORTED

CLASSIFICATION
OF PROBLEM

Problems in Agency Support
of Self-Help Groups

Difficulties in Recruiting for
Self-Help Groups — 70

Keeping Self-Help Groups Alive — 54

Community Hostile to Self-Help Group — 20

Financing — 79

—for Work with Self-Help Group — 44

—for Self-Help Group Itself — 35

Other — 52

(involving seventy-nine self-help groups) problem was financing -- either for the agency work with the group (forty-four) or the group's overall financing (thirty-five). Difficulties in recruiting for the group (indicated seventy times) was the next most noted problem. Keeping the group alive was noted by fifty-four agencies, as was inadequate group leadership. Surprisingly, among the least noted problems were auspices and control (nineteen times) and competition between the group and agency service program (eleven).

The total number of problems for each of the three groupings did not confirm the literature's stress on the difficulty of relationships between agencies and self-help groups. The highest number (302) was for problems in support of the group -- natural enough, since this classification included three of the four most mentioned categories. Problems inherent in the group itself were the next largest category (175), while problems in the self-help group-agency relationship were least noted (a total of eighty-eight times). Admittedly, the perspective reported is that of the agencies, not the self-help groups. Nevertheless, the paucity of problems regarding the agency-group relationship vividly contradicts the literature's emphasis on the potential if not inevitability of such problems.

Current Relationships

Finally, the agencies were asked about the current state of their relationships with individual self-help groups. In two hundred and sixty-eight (83 percent) of the relationships, the agency and the group were continuing to work cooperatively. Of the fifty-three instances where cooperative work had been discontinued, twenty-eight involved mutual agreement, nine came from agency incentive, and four involved group incentive. In ten instances, the self-help group was no longer functioning.

To analyze survey findings regarding auspices, objectives, services provided, and problems encountered in the relationships between groups and agencies, it was necessary to categorize the self-help groups reported.* In addition to analysis by broad group objectives, the self-help groups were ordered by the problems or phenomena on which they focused. A fifteen-part classification resulted (number of groups in parentheses):

Social Action (35) Groups primarily are outward and community-focused. They include tenants' associations, school groups, day care groups, and food banks.

Weight (8) Stress individuals' obesity problems.

Money (4) Emphasize individuals' financial problems.

Alcohol (40) Cover alcoholism as it affects victims and their family members.

Adoption/Foster Care (19) Stress advocacy for and the difficulties involved in the use of these services.

Violence (73) Focus primarily on familial violence including child abuse.

Physical Handicap/Illness (22) Concern for those problems in terms of the afflicted and their families.

Grief (28) Deal with the phenomena of loss.

Psychiatric (5) Focus on phobias and other psy-

---

*Three hundred forty-two self-help groups had enough information for this classification.

chiatric problems.

Immigrant Refugee (10) Concerned with the situations faced by new immigrants and refugees. They generally are ethnic specific.

Divorce (19) Deal with the problems of divorce.

Single Parent (27) Emphasize situations faced by single parents.

General Parenting (17) Focus on the challenges of raising children but do not emphasize the single parent aspect.

Women's (14) Concerned with problems specific to women.

Other Support (21) Catch-all category covering other groups whose problems (for example, older parents, student needs, gay identification) are dealt with primarily through one-on-one support.

Thus classified, the groups ranged in size from four or 1 percent (money) to seventy-three or 21 percent (violence). Collectively, the five largest categories (violence, alcohol, social action, grief, and single parent) made up nearly three-fifths (59 percent) of the total.

The number of groups in the violence category is not surprising. Many of these were Parents Anonymous groups. Such groups frequently seek out family service agency support. Further, prevention of family violence is a key focus of family service agencies.

Most listings in the single parent category were Parents Without Partners groups. As in the case of Alcoholics Anonymous, the relatively uniform structure of this kind of group may make it easier for agencies to relate to it.

Social action was the third largest group. However, it was the only one that by definition has a primarily outward, societal focus. Considering the number and variety of advocacy groups, neighborhood organizations, and consumer groups, more such representation might have been expected.

The relative scarcity of groups dealing with physical handicap and illness and with foster care and adoption is notable. Gartner and Reissman report that almost every illness has engendered a self-help group. As adoption becomes more prevalent -- especially the adoption of hard-to-place children -- an increase in adoptive self-help groups may occur.

Somewhat surprising was the lack of psychiatric groups. The increased use of mental health services and the phenomena of deinstitutionalization should have resulted in large numbers of self-help groups in this area relating to agencies.

The number of women's groups seems low at first glance. However, women's issues also may have been covered in other types of groups such as those dealing with violence, divorce, and single parenthood. The same observation may be made regarding general parenting groups; their issues may be covered in other self-help groups. However, the increase in parenting groups (for example, Tough Love) with whom family service agencies may have philosophical differences could account for the relatively low representation.

The lack of groups concerned with the phenomena of aging is interesting. The elderly are the most rapidly increasing segment of the United States and Canadian populations. They are group-minded and have formed large numbers of local, regional, and national organizations. However, they clearly are not relating to local family service agencies.

Finally, agencies covered in the survey seem to have a mixed pattern of relationships with survival-oriented groups whose members are discriminated against or are labeled deviant. Family service agencies may be expected to relate to such groups if they are approached and if the emphasis is on client problems (Parents Anonymous, for example). However, they do not seem to have contacts with groups (for example, homosexuals and former prisoners) which stress esteem and societal acceptance.

Table 5 presents the categories of self-help groups by their objectives. Three hundred and thirty-five groups could be so classified. As noted earlier, 86 percent of the groups focused on individual member's problems. In only two classifications, psychiatric and single parent, did less than half of the groups stress such concerns. In nine classifications -- including the two largest, violence and alcohol -- three-fourths or more of the reported groups emphasized individual's problems. In all but one category -- single parents -- individual member's problems are reported by a majority or plurality. Even in the social action category, it is the most noted objective.

Forty-eight percent of all the groups emphasized self improvement rather than more specific problems. In four categories -- weight, immigrant/refugees, divorce, and single parents -- over 60 percent of the groups stressed this objective.

Support of a way of life or a philosophy was stressed by a total of 34 percent of the self-help groups. In only three categories (weight, alcohol, adoption/foster care) did 60 percent or more of reported groups stress this area.

TABLE 5
CATEGORIES OF SELF-HELP GROUPS BY OBJECTIVES

CATEGORIES OF SELF-HELP GROUPS	OBJECTIVES							
	INDIVIDUAL MEMBERS		SELF-IMPROVEMENT		SUPPORT WAY OF LIFE		SOCIAL CHANGE	
	NUMBER	(%)	NUMBER	(%)	NUMBER	(%)	NUMBER	(%)
Social Action	26	(74)	15	(43)	11	(31)	22	(63)
Weight	7	(87)	7	(87)	6	(75)	3	(37)
Money	3	(75)	1	(25)	2	(50)	2	(50)
Alcohol	40	(100)	19	(47)	27	(67)	13	(33)
Adoption/ Foster Care	11	(58)	9	(47)	12	(63)	6	(32)
Violence	72	(99)	29	(40)	11	(15)	15	(21)
Physical/Handi-cap/Illness	21	(95)	9	(41)	5	(23)	6	(27)
Grief	26	(93)	7	(25)	3	(11)	6	(21)
Psychiatric	2	(40)	2	(40)	1	(20)	2	(40)
Immigrant/ Refugee	9	(90)	8	(80)	5	(50)	3	(30)
Divorce	17	(89)	12	(63)	8	(42)	4	(21)
Single Parent	12	(44)	18	(67)	6	(22)	6	(22)
General Parenting	17	(100)	7	(41)	3	(18)	4	(24)
Women	10	(71)	8	(57)	5	(36)	5	(36)
Other Support	15	(71)	11	(52)	9	(43)	7	(33)
TOTAL	288	(86)	162	(48)	114	(34)	104	(31)

Aggregately, the least noted self-help group objective was intervention to change social conditions. In only one category, social action, was it attributed to more than three-fifths of the groups reported.

In considering these figures, it is necessary to keep in mind that the agencies reporting their relationships with the self-help groups were family service agencies. As such, they tended to favor certain objectives. In addition, self-help groups within a community have preconceptions of the interests of the family service agencies in that community and are likely to decide on whether to relate to them in the light of those preconceptions.

Family service agencies' primary focus is on specific problems of individuals and families. They tend to relate most readily to self-help groups concerned with the problems of individual members and such groups would be most likely to gravitate to them.

The objective of self improvement, by itself, is less related to the focus of family service agencies. However, as indicated in Table 4, they work with self-help groups stressing self improvement if these groups also emphasize individual member's problems.

Backing for a philosophy or a way of life is not an emphasis of family service agencies. They may be amenable to work with self-help groups stressing a philosophy or way of life if that philosophy or lifestyle (sobriety, moderation in eating, or adoption, for example) has community acceptance.

In the last twenty years family service agencies have developed considerable interest in social

conditions, realizing individual and family problems frequently result from these conditions. As
will be seen, they have supported the formation of
self-help groups stressing social action. Their
reputation, however, is not as social action agencies, and groups stressing social change may see
agencies as irrelevant to their goals.

Origin of Groups

The survey produced data that made possible the
categorizing of self-help groups according to how
they were organized. As Table 6 shows, a plurality
(46 percent) of groups reported were organized by
their participants. Over two-thirds of weight,
alcohol, adoption/foster care, psychiatric, and
single-parent groups fell into this category.

About one-third of the groups were organized by
their local family service agency. Women's, other
support, general parenting, divorce, grief, and
social action groups were most likely to be under
this auspice. Psychiatric, alcohol, and single-
parent groups were least likely to be.

Only 23 percent of all self-help groups were
organized through the auspices of another organization. Money and physical handicap/illness groups
were the categories most noted under this auspice;
no adoption/foster care groups were so organized.

Among the five most frequently reported types of
self-help groups, three -- single parents, alcoholism, and violence -- were likely to be sponsored
independently while the other two -- social action
and grief -- were most often founded by a local
family service agency.

The pattern of sponsorship has logical explanations. The founders of alcohol problem and single
parent groups can draw on the experience and
formats of Alcoholics Anonymous and Parents Without

TABLE 6
CATEGORIES OF SELF-HELP GROUPS BY HOW ORGANIZED (AUSPICE)

CATEGORIES OF SELF-HELP GROUPS	ORGANIZED UNDER AGENCY AUSPICE		ORGANIZED UNDER AUSPICE OF ANOTHER GROUP		ORGANIZED INDEPEN-DENTLY		TOTAL*	
	NUMBER	(%)	NUMBER	(%)	NUMBER	(%)	NUMBER	(%)
Social Action	15	(43)	8	(23)	12	(34)	35	(100)
Weight	1	(13)	1	(13)	6	(75)	8	(101)
Money	1	(33)	2	(67)	0	(-)	3	(100)
Alcohol	1	(3)	10	(29)	23	(68)	34	(100)
Adoption Foster/Care	5	(31)	0	(-)	11	(69)	16	(100)
Violence	21	(30)	24	(34)	25	(36)	70	(100)
Physical Handicap/Illness	3	(23)	6	(46)	4	(31)	13	(100)
Grief	12	(44)	5	(19)	10	(37)	27	(100)
Psychiatric	0	(-)	1	(25)	3	(75)	4	(100)
Immigrant/Refugee	3	(30)	1	(10)	6	(60)	10	(100)
Divorce	8	(44)	3	(17)	7	(39)	18	(100)
Single Parent	3	(12)	2	(8)	21	(81)	26	(101)
General Parenting	7	(44)	3	(19)	6	(37)	16	(100)
Women	9	(64)	2	(14)	3	(21)	14	(99)
Other Support	11	(52)	3	(14)	7	(33)	21	(99)
TOTAL	100	(32)	71	(23)	144	(46)	315	(101)

*Only Self-Help Groups for which a response was noted are included.

Partners to get started. Parenting has always been an area of involvement of family service agencies, and women's concerns, coping with grief, and social action have become issues of interest. Local agencies would be sensitive to these needs and form groups in these areas. Physical handicap/illness groups need both formats and a flow of information on the handicap/illness of their focus. They tend to look at larger organizations that can fulfill these needs for sponsorship.

As noted, seventy-two of the reporting agencies worked with two or more self-help groups. In addition to this information, the survey provided data to answer researcher interest in whether agencies with multiple arrangements concentrated on one or two types of groups or worked with a wide selection. It might be expected that agencies successful in working with one type of self-help group (those focused on alcohol, for example) would tend toward relationships with other groups in the same category. Agencies would be able to utilize their experience and contacts with their first group in relating to similar groups.

Using the fifteen-category breakdown of self-help groups, the survey team found that only seven of the agencies with more than one self-help group contact worked exclusively with one category. Of these seven, three worked exclusively with groups focused on violence and one each was related to self-help groups emphasizing alcohol, social action, general parenting, and divorce.

On the other hand, forty-one of the seventy-two agencies did focus primarily on certain types of self-help groups and reported multiple groups within the same categories. Agencies were most likely to work with multiple groups within the violence (sixteen agencies), alcohol (nine agencies), adoption (five agencies), divorce (five agencies), and social action (five agencies) categories.

Problems-Services Ratio

Table 7 depicts the average number of services and problems encountered by agencies in relating to each of the categories of self-help groups; it also shows the ratio of problems to services. Overall, an average of 3.7 services was received from agencies by reported self-help groups. The lowest average number of services was received by alcohol (1.8 services) and weight (2.5) groups. Women's (4.9), grief (4.6), adoption/foster care (4.5), and social action (4.4) groups received the most services.

Agencies reported an average 1.5 problems per self-help group. Immigrant and refugee (2.3 problems), social action (2.1), and other support (2.0) groups were most likely to have problems reported. Alcohol (0.4), general parenting (0.4) and adoption/foster care (1.1) groups were least likely to have problems reported.

The number of services and problems are graphed by group in Chart 6. Two categories, alcohol and divorce, were below average in both problems and services, with alcohol well below in both areas. The weight, single parent, and money categories were below average in services but average or slightly above in problems. The physical handicap/ illness, grief, adoption/foster care, and general parenting categories were below average in problems but involved a higher than average number of services from family service agencies. Most surprising, almost half of the categories, including two of the largest (women, psychiatric, violence, social action, immigrants and refugees, other support) are above average in both services and problems with agencies.

The ratio of problems to services averaged .40.

TABLE 7
<u>CATEGORIES OF SELF-HELP GROUPS BY AVERAGE NUMBER OF SERVICES OFFERED, PROBLEMS
NOTED BY AGENCIES, AND RATIO OF PROBLEMS TO SERVICES</u>

CATEGORIES OF SELF-HELP GROUPS	AVERAGE NUMBER OF SERVICES	AVERAGE NUMBER OF PROBLEMS	RATIO OF PROBLEMS TO SERVICES
Social Action	4.4	2.1	.48
Weight	2.5	1.8	.72
Money	3.3	1.5	.45
Alcohol	1.8	0.4	.22
Adoption/Foster Care	4.5	1.1	.24
Violence	4.0	1.9	.48
Physical Handicap/Illness	3.8	1.4	.37
Grief	4.6	1.4	.30
Psychiatric	4.0	1.8	.45
Immigrant/Refugee	3.8	2.3	.61
Divorce	3.0	1.2	.40
Single Parent	3.0	1.5	.50
General Parenting	3.7	0.4	.11
Women	4.9	1.9	.39
Other Support	3.8	2.0	.53
Overall Average	3.7	1.5	.40

59

CHART 6
CATEGORIES OF GROUPS BY AVERAGE NUMBER OF SERVICES AND PROBLEMS

Type of Group

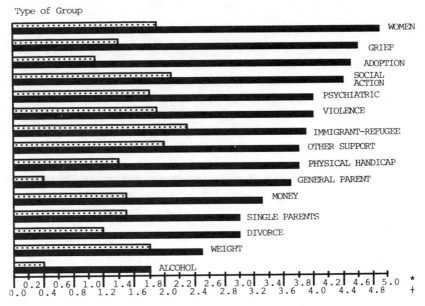

Average Number of Problems or Services

 AVERAGE NUMBER OF PROBLEMS

 AVERAGE NUMBER OF SERVICES

*   PROBLEMS

\+   SERVICES

Significantly higher ratios were noted for weight, immigrant, other support, and single parent groups. Lower ratios were found with general parenting, alcohol, adoption/foster care, and grief groups.

From a hard-headed planning viewpoint this observation is puzzling. Agencies seem to become involved with groups to which they offer a greater than average number of services or which pose more than average problems for them. A number of explanations can be offered for this phenomenon.

The most simple explanation is that agencies may not know what they are getting into when they commence a relationship with a self-help group. Such relationships may be initiated without much planning or weighing of consequences. Even if boundaries were originally set, they may stretch as the relationship develops. Once a relationship is established, it may not be analyzed as to cost; habit may keep it going.

In addition, there may be factors that override the cost aspect of an agency-group relationship. Agencies may feel that their mandate requires that they relate to certain types of groups. Many agencies see social action as an area in which they should be involved, even though social action groups are above average in problems and services. Agencies may be asked by groups -- Parents Anonymous, for example -- to relate to them. Finally, agency executives may discount the immediate costs of self-help groups because of the larger goal of broadening their agencies' clientele, expertise, and influence.

How Much of a Burden?

How much of an extra burden do service- and problem-intensive groups put on agencies? The study indicates that even the most demanding category of self-help groups utilized fewer than five

services. The most problematic averaged slightly
more than two problems. As services increased, so
did problems. However, the ratio of increase, .40,
was relatively low. On the average, an agency had
to offer 2.5 additional services before it encountered one additional problem. Agencies may be
willing to pay this cost.

Since the three service categories -- low, medium, and high interaction/communication -- differ in
their actual number of services, they can best be
compared by looking at the percentage of potential
services actually given by the reporting agencies.
Each category has a potential number of services
that can be offered to self-help groups. For example, the high interaction/communication category
has three potential services.

Table 8 provides a summary of the percentage of
potential services in the three categories that was
actually given to self-help groups by agencies. It
compares the percentage of potential services
offered over the fifteen categories of self-help
groups.

Some groups (alcohol, weight, single parent)
frequently utilized low level but seldom used medium and high level services. Referring to Table 7,
they received a low average number of services from
and had relatively few problems with agencies.
These groups tended to be formed independently.
They utilized relatively set formats and the experience of other groups in their provision of
services. This kind of self-help group probably
does not need as much help from agencies as other
groups. The primary role of the agency may be
referral.

Other types of groups were above average in the
use of all categories of services or of medium and
high level services. They included women's, adop-

TABLE 8

CATEGORIES OF GROUPS BY PERCENTAGE OF POTENTIAL SERVICES IN EACH OF THREE
SERVICE GROUPINGS ACTUALLY GIVEN BY AGENCIES

	SERVICE LEVEL		
CATEGORIES OF GROUPS	LOW INTERACTION/ COMMUNICATION %	MEDIUM INTERACTION/ COMMUNICATION %	HIGH INTERACTION/ COMMUNICATION %
Social Action	43	37	54
Weight	87	15	25
Money	50	21	33
Alcohol	77	7	10
Adoption/Foster Care	89	35	49
Violence	60	28	49
Physical Handicap/Illness	64	27	38
Grief	61	35	54
Psychiatric	80	27	47
Immigrant/Refugee	90	22	47
Divorce	47	17	42
Single Parent	85	20	32
General Parenting	59	36	59
Women	86	31	59
Other Support	52	29	47
Overall Average Percentage of Potential Problems Noted	67	26	43

tion/foster care, social action, grief, violence, general parenting, and other support groups. Again, as indicated in Table 7, these categories used the greatest number of services. They had relatively few problems with their relationship with agencies.

These groups are more likely to be formed by family service agencies. They relate to issues (parenting, family violence, adoption) most immediately within the realm of family service agencies or issues (women, grief, community action) with which family service agencies would like to become more involved.

Overall, agencies in the survey offered 67 percent of potential low interaction/communication services (referrals) to self-help groups. They were most likely to refer to immigrant and refugees, adoption/foster care, weight, women's, and single parent's groups and least likely to refer to social action, divorce, and money groups.

In total, the agencies provided 26 percent of potential medium level interaction/communication services to self-help groups. They offered the highest percentage of such services to social action, general parenting, adoption/foster care, and grief oriented groups. The groups receiving the lowest percentage of such services include alcohol, weight, and divorce groups.

Over all, the agencies provided a surprisingly large 43 percent of potential high interaction/communication services to self-help groups. The services were provided to nearly three-fifths of the general parenting and women's groups and over one-half of the social action and grief groups. However, they were given to less than a third of the alcohol, weight, single parent, and money groups.

The premier subgroup within the high interaction/communication category was agency leadership of the self-help groups. Overall, 24 percent of groups were provided with this kind of leadership. More than half of the women's and general parenting and nearly half of the grief self-help groups were led in this manner. None of the money, alcohol, psychiatric, and single parents groups were.

As the intensity of agency services to self-help groups increased, it might be expected that their quantity would decrease. A greater percentage of potential low interaction/communication services should be offered than medium interaction/communication services. Similarly, a higher percentage of intermediate as opposed to high services should be offered. This is logical from an administrative viewpoint since agencies should be better able to offer the commitment of time and resources needed for low and medium level relations as opposed to high level relations.

However, the survey figures show agencies offering proportionately more low and high level services than medium level services. Such level of involvement raises questions about problems between agencies and self-help groups, which will be covered in the next chapter.

Table 9 looks at the three categories of problems (inherent in the self-help group, in relating to the group, and in supporting the group) reported by agencies. It records the number and percentage of potential problems with the self-help group that were actually noted by agencies and compares it across the categories of self-help groups.

Over all three categories, the number of problems noted in the survey was quite small -- 10 percent of potential problems.

TABLE 9

CATEGORIES OF GROUPS BY PERCENTAGE OF POTENTIAL PROBLEMS IN EACH OF THREE
CATEGORIES ACTUALLY NOTED BY AGENCIES

CATEGORIES OF GROUPS	PROBLEMS INHERENT IN GROUP %	PROBLEMS IN GROUP-AGENCY RELATIONSHIP %	PROBLEMS IN AGENCY SUPPORT FOR GROUPS %
Social Action	17	2	23
Weight	20	3	16
Money	25	0	0
Alcohol	2	2	7
Adoption/Foster Care	8	5	8
Violence	14	4	26
Physical Handicap/Illness	14	7	10
Grief	15	4	12
Psychiatric	20	2	10
Immigrant/Refugee	10	16	18
Divorce	7	3	11
Single Parent	15	7	9
General Parenting	6	0	15
Women	16	3	18
Other Support	17	9	14
Overall Average Percentage of Potential Problems Noted	13.7	4.5	13.1

Problems inherent in the self-help group itself were most mentioned, with an overall 13.7 percent of potential problems. They were most frequent with money and weight groups and least common with alcohol and general parenting groups.

Close behind (13.1 percent of potential problems noted) were problems in providing support for the self-help group. With its focus on impediments to aiding the groups, this was probably the most positive of the problem categories. This type of problem was most often noted with violence and social action groups and least mentioned with money and alcohol groups.

Agencies' problems in relating to self-help groups were the least noted (4 percent of potential problems recorded). Only in one category (immigrants and refugees) were more than 10 percent of potential problems indicated.

Based on survey data, the number and level of services offered to a category of self-help groups does not seem to have been related to the number of problems the agencies report. Referring to Table 7, low service groups (alcohol, weight, single parents) averaged only slightly fewer problems (1.23) than groups receiving greater quantity and quality of services (women, adoption/foster care, social action, grief, violence, general parenting, other support). These latter groups averaged 1.54 problems. Further, the ratio of problems to services was higher than average for some low service groups (weight, single parents) and lower for some high service groups (general parenting, adoption/ foster care, grief).

The survey team wanted to know more about self-help groups that discontinued their relationships to agencies. Of all the groups reported, there were fifty-four situations (or 15 percent of the total number of groups reported) where cooperative work had been discontinued. In ten of these situations the groups were no longer functioning. Relationships between agencies and forty-four still existing groups had been terminated, in most instances (twenty-eight) by mutual agreement.

Agencies reported more problems (an average of 2.1 for discontinued versus 1.4 for active) with discontinued groups and gave them a slightly higher number of services (4.1 versus 3.8 for still active groups). Turning to problems, Table 10 compares the problems noted by agencies with continuing and discontinued groups. Overall, 24 percent of the problems noted were with the discontinued groups, which made up 18 percent of the total number of groups. However, in the overdependence category, nearly half (48 percent) of the problems noted were with discontinued groups. Terminated groups were also noted in 43 percent of the problems revolving around inappropriate activities. They were much less likely than the average to have been noted as having problems regarding activity demanded of participants, competition, difficulties over ethics/ideology, and community hostility.

Discontinuing Contact

Chart 7, focusing on discontinuance and auspice, indicates that agency-sponsored groups had the highest rate of discontinuance, while independently formed groups had the lowest. To some degree this might be expected, since the agencies surveyed hope that groups they start will become increasingly independent. By design, a group may ultimately discontinue its relationship with an agency.

Interviews with staff members and administrators at seven agencies (to be reported in full in the following chapter) brought out several other factors which should be considered in looking at the breaking of relations between agencies and groups

TABLE 10
PROBLEMS NOTED BY AGENCIES FOR DISCONTINUED AND CONTINUING GROUPS

PROBLEMS	DISCONTINUED GROUPS		CONTINUING GROUPS		TOTAL	
	NUMBER	(%)	NUMBER	(%)	NUMBER	(%)
Too Much/Little Activity Demanded of Participants	2	(10)	18	(90)	20	(100)
Activities Inappropriate for Most Members	3	(43)	4	(57)	7	(100)
Inadequate Group Leadership	17	(33)	35	(67)	52	(100)
Problems in Nature of Partici- pation by Group Members	6	(15)	34	(85)	40	(100)
Difficulties in Group Cohesion	14	(33)	28	(67)	42	(100)
Problems with Auspices/Control	4	(25)	12	(75)	16	(100)
Competition Between Self-Help Groups and Agency	0	(-)	8	(100)	8	(100)
Overdependence on Agency	12	(48)	13	(52)	25	(100)
Difficulties over Ethics/ Ideology	1	(10)	9	(90)	10	(100)
Lack of Coordination Between Self-Help Groups and Agencies	3	(23)	10	(77)	13	(100)
Difficulties in Recruiting for Self-Help Groups	15	(23)	49	(77)	64	(100)
Keeping Self-Help Groups Alive	15	(30)	35	(70)	50	(100)
Community Hostile to Self- Help Groups	2	(11)	16	(89)	18	(100)
Financing	15	(20)	60	(80)	75	(100)
Other	7	(14)	43	(86)	50	(100)
Overall Problem Breakdown	116	(24)	374	(76)	490	(100)

CHART 7
CONTINUING/DISCONTINUING RELATIONSHIP WITH AGENCY BY AUSPICE

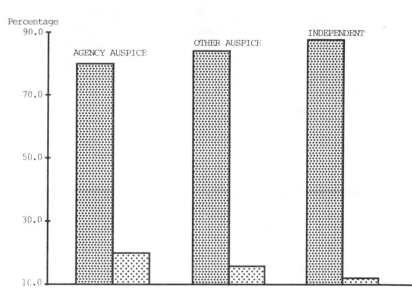

Percentage

AUSPICE

CONTINUING RELATIONS WITH AGENCY

DISCONTINUED RELATIONS WITH AGENCY

and the actual dissolution of groups.

The first of these is the issue of agency responsibility and group autonomy. Describing the time factor in agency responsibility, one agency staff member said, "We continue with a group as long as the members want or allow us to be there, as long as there is a productive relationship." Other agency-group relationships may be time-limited by agreement, discontinuing when the group becomes autonomous and self-sustaining. However, the study indicated that criteria for determining need and autonomy generally are lacking.

Another question is how much an agency should influence the natural flow and ebb of self-help groups. Such groups, sustained by their members' commitment, are fluid to the degree that that commitment changes. Individuals who join a group during a personal crisis may leave the group after working out the problem. If most members no longer have the need for a group, it may have fulfilled its purpose and possibly should be discontinued. However, other people, non-members, may be going through the same sort of problem and need the group. One agency worker questioned how much effort an agency should put into recruiting members for a self-help group or keeping it alive in anticipation of future needs.

Individual professionals within agencies start or develop contacts with self-help groups. When these professionals leave agencies, the relationships with the affected groups often deteriorate.

Issues raised in interviews with agency workers produced more questions than answers. With some exceptions, the answers reflected less than fully-formed agency policies on termination in particular and on self-help groups in general.

5

IN-DEPTH INTERVIEWS

The in-depth interviews supplemented the questionnaires and provided valuable information about
the relationships between self-help groups and
human service agencies. Seven agencies were
selected for this part of the study. Each was
connected with at least five self-help groups. In
addition to adding more detailed responses to the
items covered in the questionnaire, the interviews
provided insights into the philosophy and decision-
making process behind establishing contracts with
groups, how relationships evolved with the passing
of time, and the effect on ties between groups and
agencies of outside factors and individual person-
alities.

The national organization staff person who con-
ducted the interviews visited the cooperating agencies. She met with agency administrators and staff
members and at least one person from each group
related to an agency. In addition, she attended
meetings of the groups.

Agency staff members were asked about their
working definitions of self-help groups, individual
policy regarding the groups (notably the process of
deciding which groups to relate to and on what
level), working arrangements between agencies and
groups, and the pluses and minuses of such relationships. The contacts with group members also

focused on the advantages and disadvantages of relationships with agencies.

Although the national organization had defined self-help groups for its member agencies when it sent out the questionnaires, it was interested in the agencies' own definitions. It was aware that the definitions might affect policy toward and relations with self-help groups.

In general, agencies agreed that self-help groups were open-ended, ongoing, and supportive in nature. Members' commitment was of key importance; members determined the agenda and direction of their group. The leadership of the group could come from professionals or lay persons. Self-help generally was seen as performing preventive -- especially in stress alleviation -- and maintenance functions.

Most of the conflict among agencies over definition came in regard to the therapeutic role -- or lack of it -- of self-help groups. Some agencies emphasized that self-help was, at best, an adjunct to therapy. They noted that self-help might be the first step in an individual's progress to needed therapy. Some saw self-help as important for people who had completed therapy; however, they felt that therapy on any level was beyond the capabilities of self-help groups, even those with professional advisors from agencies.

Other agencies viewed self-help groups, especially those with professional guidance, as having the potential to fulfill some therapeutic functions. They frequently cited Parents Anonymous as an example of a self-help activity with therapeutic components. Parents Anonymous groups engage a sponsor (clinician) to work with peer leadership. The interaction of group members, leadership, and the clinician create a therapeutic and supportive milieu. In effect, the group provides at least part of the therapy.

No agency saw self-help groups without professional guidance and involvement as successful substitutes for therapists.

Thus the agencies interviewed defined the therapeutic role of self-help groups in a relatively narrow spectrum ranging from no role to the possibility of a limited role in certain situations with professional guidance and participation. This limited perspective certainly reflected professional concerns regarding clients' welfare. Therapy is a treatment with both potential and peril. Training, experience, and an even-handed view of the client's situation are necessary for therapy to be successful. These factors may be lacking in self-help groups. On the other hand, this role limitation for self-help groups also may reflect concern about turf. The agencies interviewed are accepted as providers of therapeutic counseling. If local informal self-help groups can perform therapeutic functions as effectively -- and at lower cost -- than agencies, the rationale for agencies is challenged.

The Decision About Involvement

The survey sought information on how agencies decided whether to become involved with self-help groups and to what extent. The national organization needed to know the factors considered in making these decisions. The interviews with agencies revealed that few of them had fully formed policies in this matter. Decisions about becoming involved with self-help groups and the nature of the involvement were made at various staff and board levels. Generally they did not utilize all available information or consider the full variety of alternatives.

In all cases, executives played an important role in the decisions. Their opinions regarding self-help in general, interest in specific groups, and inventory of the advantages and disadvantages in relating to groups all could be key factors. However, the directors dealt with a wide variety of operational and policy issues. The interviewer found that they had opinions regarding specific aspects relating to self-help groups but seldom had formed a comprehensive philosophy. One director's main concern was whether referrals should be made to any self-help group whose services the agency had not evaluated. Another wanted to reach out to a variety of self-help groups. A third was concerned primarily with the financial burdens or opportunities afforded by self-help groups. These individual opinions certainly influenced how staff members related to self-help groups, but they left many unanswered questions to staff discretion.

Individual staff members might be interested in a particular area -- divorce or grieving, for example -- and establish a group or develop a relationship with an existing group. The group then may establish a permanent relationship with an agency but outside the framework of any policy and without any real consideration of how the group fits into the agency's service scheme. Individual staff members, faced with pressing individual and family problems, may work around decisions agency directors have made regarding self-help groups. For example, some agency directors may have qualms about referring clients to unevaluated groups, but their staff, having no other available resource, may consider referrals anyhow.

In regard to developing relationships with self-help groups, interviewed agencies seldom reported considering the resources in staff and money needed for such contacts. One executive who had weighed such considerations described self-help groups as "piranhas – they tend to eat up your staff when you say 'take what you will.'"

Finally, interviewed agencies seldom involved their boards in decisions regarding self-help groups. However, in one instance, a board member with family members participating in a self-help group encouraged the agency to establish a relationship with that group.

There were notable exceptions to this rather serendipitous pattern of establishing and defining relationships with self-help groups. In one agency an advisory committee reviewed proposals for new self-help groups according to a set of criteria that included need for the group, staff resources to be used, funding, overall agency capability, and whether the group involved a duplication of services. Another agency, considering a request to establish a self-help group for bereaved parents, concluded that its staff would need additional training in group therapy and that, because of high membership turnover, such a group would need to be supported by a strong outreach and publicity component. After discussions with its board, the agency set up a committee with executive, staff, client, and referral source (doctors and funeral directors) membership. The committee dealt with the issues involved, defined agency participation, and set up what has proven to be a very successful group.

Types of Professional Assistance

In contrast to the literature which stresses the need for self-help groups to remain separate and independent from formal service providers, the agencies interviewed said that the groups with which they interacted wanted positive professional involvement. This involvement might be expressed through a variety of professional roles. The role most often mentioned was that of facilitator for the group. One agency defined a facilitator as "a catalyst, respecting, recognizing, defining, supporting, utilizing, and preserving participant initiative and group autonomy."

Agencies said that the facilitator role was most often actualized through professionals acting as leaders within self-help groups. They pointed out three problems to be overcome by any staff member acting as a group leader. Ironically, the first problem is a worker's therapeutic skills. One agency worker commented that clinical skills get in the way of the facilitator role because "They (therapists) expect too much." Workers need to expand beyond a clinical perspective and focus on concrete issues to be effective facilitators. The second problem is that there is no one, precisely defined, role for facilitators. The role depends on the group. Self-help groups have different problems, motivations, and levels of sophistication. A facilitator must learn to be different things to different groups. The final problem is role change over time. The facilitator may be more or less of a leader as member leadership emerges and drops out. His or her roles will depend on the stage of the group's development.

Another role for professionals that was noted by the agencies is that of complementing peer leadership in a self-help group. Such a role may be time-limited or open-ended. The best example of this kind of relationship is found in Parents Anonymous groups. The sponsor role in these situations defines the agency worker as a resident clinician within the group, a clarifier of issues, and a source of professional knowledge on parenting and child abuse. However, the sponsor must respect the principle of never doing for group members what they can do for themselves. In Parents Anonymous terms, this means that certain duties always are left for the peer leadership and members. One

agency professional added that the sponsor is usually the constant who keeps the group going since
peer leadership within the group may change frequently. Of course, this role assumes that individuals will emerge within the group who are ready
and willing to assume peer leadership. Without
such leadership, the group's dependency on the
professional may grow to the point that the group
is disrupted if the professional leaves, by plan or
otherwise.

In both exclusive and shared leadership roles,
the professional also is a liaison between the
agency and the self-help group. He or she relates
the agency's perspective, agendas, values, and
goals to the group. The professional advocates to
the agency for issues of importance to the group.
On a broader level, he or she relates public opinion (of which self-help groups are one element) to
the agency. Describing this liaison relationship,
one professional said, "I go out to the community
and keep my ear to the ground and then follow up on
what I hear."

A third, more removed, professional role is that
of training indigenous leadership. Self-help
groups may not want an agency worker to play a
leadership role yet feel comfortable with a training program. One interviewed agency had developed
a six-week basic training course for self-help
group leaders. The course covered the needs of
group members, leadership functions, communications
skills, acculturation of new members, and problem-
solving techniques.

Agencies' provision of training (in leadership,
group dynamics, or other aspects of heading a
group) to group leaders has two potential benefits.
Considering the transitory nature of the groups
and their leadership, training can produce a re-
plenishing flow of leaders for new and established

groups. Further, experienced leaders of groups have noted that training could serve as refresher courses for them. They observed that an "update" course would allow them to think through their experiences as group leaders, share them with others, and incorporate them into future activities. One agency had started such a course on a trial basis.

Interviewed agencies saw their staff members in the more distant role of representing the agency to self-help groups. They perceived staff members not as counselors for groups but rather as educators telling about the agency and its services. An example of this role would be an agency that provided lectures at Parents Without Partners meetings.

Finally, agencies discussed the administrative role that they frequently play in their relations with self-help groups. The leadership, goals, and even services of the groups are changeable. Connection with an agency adds an element of permanence. In relating to groups, agencies play certain roles and have the potential to play others. For example, an agency may provide counseling backup but add recruiting efforts if the group begins to lose members.

Advantages of Relationships

The seven agencies that were interviewed were asked about the advantages and disadvantages in relating to self-help groups. They generally were quite positive about the relationships. Such a response might be expected because they were chosen on the basis of the extent and variety of their contact with self-help groups. However, the agencies also made perceptive comments about the disadvantages in relationships.

Looking on the positive side, agencies saw self-help groups as important ways of reaching out to their environment. One said that self-help groups allowed them to influence and impact on their community. Another noted that contacts resulted in positive publicity for the agency.

The groups were seen as a source of clients by the agencies. This may reflect the opinion of some agencies that groups are a precursor to therapy for many clients. As noted, agencies frequently serve as professional backup for the problems of individual group members.

Self-help groups also were seen as sources of agency volunteers. This is an interesting example of a concrete way that the groups can help to balance their exchange of services, time, and resources with family service agencies.

Agencies interviewed frequently noted that, through self-help groups, their staff members were able to broaden their knowledge of special situations and populations. One agency said that its professionals had improved their understanding of the stages a divorced person goes through from involvement with Parents Without Partners.

Finally, most agencies admitted that in some situations self-help groups were the treatment of choice.

Disadvantages of Relationships
Describing the negative aspects of relating to self-help groups, the agencies tended to center on problems inherent in the groups rather than on the groups' relationship with agencies.

One problem noted was the tendency of groups to move toward providing therapy. As mentioned earlier, the agencies had serious doubts as to self-help groups' capabilities in this area.

Self-help groups require some mutual identification on the part of members -- an identification that often involves admission of a problem. Agencies remarked that recruiting for groups might be stymied because individuals were afraid to be labeled with problems.

Self-help groups are fluid and transient. Members leave when they solve their problems and new members with similar problems enter. Agencies saw two complications resulting from this phenomenon. The first concerned bonding -- the development of identity and support among group members. One agency person noted that bonding took at least eight weeks to occur. In some types of groups (incest-focused, for example), a longer period is needed. If most members leave before bonding occurs, the group does not realize its self-helping potentials. The second phenomenon, cliques, is the result of bonding. Once group members are bonded, they are reluctant to admit newcomers. Newcomers to a group may feel excluded from its inner workings and support.

Agencies observed that variations in the responsibility and commitment of group members may cause conflict. One agency said that in a tenants' association with which it related, some members took on so much responsibility that they burned out and left, while other members did nothing and were a drag on the whole group. People have a variety of motivations for joining self-help groups. They may be unwilling or unable to meet group demands. Members referred to Parents Anonymous by family courts are reported as resenting the obligation involved. The need of members of Alcoholics Anonymous to be constantly available to support other members was noted as being too much responsibility for some individuals. Some agencies complained that members of Parents Without Partners see group meetings as places to meet members of the opposite sex rather than as occasions to work on the problems of parenting alone.

The issues of autonomy and dependency in relating with self-help groups were noted by most interviewed agencies. Even though most agencies did not report specific problems with autonomy, they seemed sensitive toward this area, especially in terms of agencies impinging on the autonomy and changing the nature of self-help groups. Agencies also were concerned about over-dependency. One agency noted that many individuals had had negative experiences with professionals and that when they found one they liked (through an agency-group relationship) they "hang on for dear life." Finally, one agency mentioned the logical connection between autonomy and dependency. It noted that over-dependence in a group may result from a professional who identifies with the group and (perhaps unconsciously) encourages dependency so that the relationship will continue.

Several agencies mentioned multiplying demands from self-help groups. Like most organizations, self-help groups will utilize resources where they can get them. If an agency is relatively open-ended in its commitment of resources, it may find itself being taken advantage of.

In-Put from Groups

The researcher's visits to member agencies included attendance at a number of meetings of self-help groups with which the agencies were related. Each of these groups received high level inter-action/communication services and had a worker assigned to it. Self-help group leaders were asked about their groups and the groups' relations with the agencies. Their comments were exclusively positive both about the groups and the agencies.

Self-help groups were described as providing
formats in which members could feel safe in venti-
lating their emotions, where they could learn about
themselves and others, and where they could be
assured of a supportive atmosphere. An elder peer
counseling group member commented that "I'm nobody
by myself." Growing confidence, giving up manipu-
lative behavior, and combating hostility from the
outside world were noted as benefits of self-help
groups. A member of a single parent group of
public assistance mothers said that she and others
were able to cut through the back-stabbing common
among many welfare recipients because of the inti-
macy they had developed in the group. Finally,
self-help group leaders said that they had been
able to develop better, more personal relationships
with professionals because of experience in a
group.

When self-help leaders described their groups'
relationships with agencies, they concentrated on
agency workers assigned to the groups. Their comments about these workers, personally and in terms
of what they had done for the groups, were extreme-
ly positive. Group leaders and members generally
knew something about agency services but little
about agency policies -- even those related to
self-help groups.

6

IMPLICATIONS

The findings of this study of relationships between self-help groups and human service agencies can be of value to a wide range of individuals and organizations in the helping professions. For this reason, the description of the survey and the report of its outcome have been presented with as little reference as possible to the identity of the national organization that sponsored it, Family Service America. The relevance of survey method and findings is to some degree universal; the absence of specific reference to the sponsor may encourage readers to appropriate the material to their own interests.

Implications are of a different genre than facts. They are considerably less universal; a statement of them represents only one way of thinking and acting about a set of facts. The authors of this report, who prepared it for Family Service America, drew their implications in this chapter in the light of FSA's interests. Other organizations will see other implications. Hopefully, the chapter will be of value to readers as an example of how the facts may be weighed and acted upon.

The chapter focuses on several issues key to relationships between family service agencies and self-help groups. It suggests the need to develop guidelines for some of the relationships and stresses the need for further study.

Family service agencies tend to relate to self-help groups which focus on problems or phenomena within the agencies' interest and service areas. Violence, alcoholism, single parenting, and grief, to name a few, directly affect family life. While the impact of social action is both more positive and indirect, it also is an area where the involvement of family service agencies is needed.

This pattern is reinforced by the goals of self-help groups related to family service agencies. They are predominantly the personal level goals of inner focused groups.

Should family service agencies broaden their perspectives and relate to a greater variety of self-help groups? To analyze this question, it is necessary to divide the universe of self-help groups to which agencies do not relate into two parts. The first part consists of those self-help groups which focus primarily on individual and family as well as group problems. It includes groups for dischargees from psychiatric hospitals or for the elderly, groups focused on illness or adoption. The second part is those outer-focused self-help groups whose emphasis is exclusively or almost exclusively on macro level problems. It encompasses ethnic, neighborhood, and "cause" self-help groups.

Prudent family service agencies may want to expand their ties to the first part before the second. Outreach to self-help groups stressing individual and family problems would allow agencies to broaden their universe in areas where they are knowledgeable and where there apparently is a greater potential need for their services. Outreach to macro level groups might involve situations where family service agencies' knowledge and skills would be less relevant.

Family service agencies rightfully complain that they are expected to be all things to all people. An expansion to different kinds of groups -- but groups still relevant to the agencies' skills and goals -- would allow them to be more, but not all, things.

Factors Influencing Involvement

There is no overall order in how family service agencies become involved with self-help groups and no real structure to impose such order. At present, a series of factors that interact in a variety of ways determine how the agencies become involved with and relate to self-help groups. They include:

Philosophy. Agencies naturally relate to groups with whom they have no major philosophical differences.

Reputation. Agencies think they know what to expect with certain types of groups such as Alcoholics Anonymous, Parents Anonymous, and Parents Without Partners. These groups have formats and governing structures which the agencies can understand.

Experience. If an agency successfully related to a self-help group, it may support a duplicate group or groups in a similar area.

Influence. Board members, United Ways, or governing bodies may suggest initiating groups in certain areas; the agencies may feel it wise to accept their suggestions.

Population Type. Family service agencies focus on families and children. They gravitate toward establishing relations with groups serving these populations.

Services. With their emphasis on individual and family problems, agencies tend to relate to groups with similar emphasis as opposed to groups stressing self-improvement, life style, or social problems.

Culture. Agencies prefer groups culturally and linguistically similar to their present service population. Different groups (for example, immigrant/refugee groups) may be harder to work with.

Resources. Agencies which have a cushion of funding or have staff whom they can assign to serve new groups may be more amenable toward establishing contact. Similarly, the opportunity for funding may make an agency willing to relate to a self-help group.

Demands. Agencies prefer groups that at least initially pose fewer problems and make fewer demands. They favor groups that can make positive contributions to the agency.

Serendipity. A persistent client or a worker with a particular interest may influence an agency toward relations with a particular type of group.

Need. In a few situations, agencies have thought through the need for self-help groups in certain areas in their community. They then have focused their efforts on establishing relationships with these types of groups.

Planning Goals. On very rare occasions, agencies have been proactive, thinking how relations with various types of self-help groups may advance the agency's planning goals and making contacts accordingly.

Most of these factors are relevant and should be
realistically considered in planning for self-help
group involvement. The key concern, of course, is
planning. Factors should be considered in a logical manner by an established committee within an
agency before decisions are made on whether to
become involved with self-help groups and on what
level.

Lack of Medium Level Services

Family service agencies are likely to refer
clients to self-help groups. They are also likely
to offer services of a high level of interaction/
communication. The relative paucity of medium
level services is worth discussing.

Referring clients to self-help groups, a low
level service, is a set procedure demanding little
effort from an agency or its staff. High level
services -- group leadership, professional consultation, or backup -- are a modification of what the
agency and its staff members do in relationships
with individuals and families. Quite naturally,
staff members think about interpersonal service
before administration. They may not consider the
concrete, administratively based, medium level
services such as training, financing, administra-
tive/physical support, connecting/informing, orga-
nizing/recruiting, and research. If the offer of
such services to a self-help group is considered,
it may be seen as an adjunct to high level
services. For example, a group with professional
leadership might be given meeting space and copying
privileges.

With a few exceptions, agencies regard referrals
to self-help groups as not constituting endorsement. High level services for a group generally do
involve endorsement but also a great deal of influence over the group. Family service agencies

may be wary of medium level services because they
could imply endorsement of groups without providing
influence over them.

Medium level services have an inherent value.
An agency developing services for a self-help group
should consider their relevance. Medium level
services are varied but generally deal with the
areas -- training, administration, networking, and
research -- where self-help groups are weakest.
Provision of these services might allow group members to concentrate on interpersonal support.

Medium level services were an area where surveyed agencies reported some of their most innova-
tive relationships with self-help groups. One
agency developed a questionnaire through which a
group could provide feedback on issues that its
members wished to deal with. Another provided
telephone services to several groups -- a service
crucial to keeping members in touch and recruiting
new members. Several agencies trained peer group
leaders to be both role models and facilitators.
Others helped groups to write proposals for funding
and one administered state funding for several
groups.

A self-help group may need medium level services
more than counseling or leadership. A group's
overtures to a family service agency may not be a
covert request for therapy; the group may simply be
looking for a place to meet and someone to do its
books.

Some formal service providers offer space to and
list self-help groups in directories without sub-
scribing to all of their views and goals. Family
service agencies can specify that provision of
medium level services does not constitute endorsement of the groups to which they are offered.

Absence of Interchange

Family service agencies interact with self-help groups separately. There is virtually no interchange of information or experience among agencies working with groups. The survey uncovered examples of agencies trying to develop policy and program related to self-help groups without the advantage of advice or information from the national organization, other member agencies, or experts in the field.

A system for networking to facilitate the sharing of information and experience clearly is needed. Such a system could limit instances of agencies "reinventing the wheel" as they duplicate development work already done elsewhere. It also would facilitate the dissemination of models developed by both the local agencies and national organization.

Networking can be most efficiently coordinated on a national level. It involves both the dissemination of new information and models to member agencies and the development of a resource collection which member agencies can draw upon as needed.

Family Service America already has published several articles on this study of the relationships between family service agencies and self-help groups. This report will be disseminated to member agencies, and it and some examples of the agency-group relations it uncovered will be the subject of workshops at FSA-sponsored meetings. If the national organization receives funding for further study and guideline development in agency-group relations, it will publish and distribute the resulting material.

Cycles of Self-Help Groups

Self-help groups start, grow, develop, and often die. Family service agencies relating to groups have to consider seriously the issues of separation and termination.

Groups may utilize different agency services at different points in their relationships. A time may be reached when no further services are needed and separation occurs. This development may be planned -- for example, when only short-term leadership training is to be provided or when an agency starts a group with the goal of its becoming self-sufficient. Separation also may happen naturally. Family service agencies need to monitor their relationships with self-help groups to see if the services provided are still relevant. They should see separation as a potentially positive step -- both in terms of a group's development and independence and in freeing agency resources to work with other groups. In an amicable separation, an agency may remain on call, ready to offer further aid if the group requests it. An agency may ask the advice and endorsement of separated groups in establishing new relationships with other groups.

Garland and associates discuss the five stages of group development. The fifth stage is termination, the actual ending of the group. Coplon and Strull describe two types of termination in self-help groups. In the first, the group has had a constant inflow of new members and leaders. Founding members gradually terminate, but the group -- in effect a new group -- continues. In the second situation, membership in the group has remained static. Members have dealt with crises and made adaptations. The needs that the group was designed to meet no longer are relevant and the group dissolves.

Family service agencies must deal with termination on both a personal and structural level. On a personal level, the agency professional must assure group members that termination on either level is acceptable. Agency personnel must also realize that termination may be the best course of action for a group, even an indicator of its success.

On a structural level, the agency needs to understand that the first type of termination will result in a group with new leaders and members and possibly new needs. A reassessment of services and possibly negotiation with the group about service provision are called for.

If a self-help group looks as if it may dissolve, the relating family service agency has an even harder decision. Is there a further need within the community for the services of the group? If so, should the agency try to keep the group alive while it reaches out to new members? Or should it let the group dissolve and tie in with another self-help group or develop a new group?

The survey sample of terminated groups is too small to look for characteristics among them. However, termination raises several policy questions that are worthy of further study. Are groups sponsored by family service agencies or other organizations more likely to terminate than groups founded independently? If so, is termination the result of less commitment from members than is found in independently founded groups?

The Need for Standards

This study offers a picture at one point in time of the relationships between family service agencies and self-help groups. It is a confused picture that reflects a lack of order in how the agencies become involved in relations with groups. The study does not mirror the changes in agencies' relationship with groups -- in services, problems, and all other aspects of relationship -- over time. This observation indicates the need for two further kinds of endeavors in the area of relationships between family service agencies and self-help groups. The first concerns standards -- the tentative beginning of some frameworks for these relationships. The second concerns process -- the need to know more about how relationships develop and what factors and changes in groups and agencies, as well as other areas, affect that development.

One area where there is enough information to begin the development of frameworks is in the initiation of group-agency relationships. Initiation might begin with guidelines to exploring whether a local family service agency should relate on any level to self-help groups. Are such groups relevant to the agencies' goals and objectives? Is there community support for general and specific agency-group relations? Does the agency have or can it obtain the cushion of staff and resources necessary to establish and sustain relationships?

If an agency decides to relate to self-help groups, another set of questions becomes important. The agency will need to develop overall guidelines on the types of groups to which to relate. It will need a basis for deciding whether to relate to existing groups or to form its own groups. The agency will have to decide whether to outreach to self-help groups or wait for them to come to it. It will have to determine what kinds of groups to connect with. In doing so, it should review its own goals and objectives and assess community needs. Finally, the agency will have to determine the parameters of the services it will make available. It should determine both the levels of interaction/communication and the specific services it will make available.

In developing relationships with specific self-help groups, the agency will have to create individual service packages focused on what the groups need and are willing to accept and what the agency can offer. In cooperation with each group, an agency might develop a set of objectives for the relationship. These might include changing services and greater self-sufficiency for the group. The agency could create a system to review the relationship to see if goals are being met.

Participants in the application of these guidelines need to be determined. They might include agency board, director, staff, clientele, and representatives from self-help groups and the community. Key questions include who would participate in each area of decision making and where final decision-making power would lie.

Guidelines for establishing relationships with self-help groups could be developed by a combination of national and local family service staff and experts in the self-help area. These standards should be tested in a variety of different agency settings. Important variables to be considered in choosing these settings include agency size, previous relationships with self-help groups, number and variety of groups related to, and the services offered these groups. Questionnaires, interviews, and similar instruments to obtain feedback from participating agencies would be developed.

The Need for Process

The survey's in-depth interviews with seven agencies indicated that, once established, their relationships with self-help groups were fluid, changing over time. Before it can begin to develop guidelines for ongoing relationships with self-help groups, Family Service America should know more about the process of agency-group relationships, how they change, and the reasons for these changes.

The relationships of individual family service agencies and self-help groups may indicate a varying pattern of services asked for, offered, and utilized. Changes may be reflected in the number, types, and combination of services.

Variations in services may indicate a change in the self-help group's needs, either as expressed by the group itself or as seen by the agency. They may also indicate shifts in what the agency can or will provide for the self-help group. Changes may be planned (as in a situation where family service agencies encourage self-help groups they have founded to become more autonomous) or made in reaction to new circumstances.

The types and combinations of problems between agencies and groups may alter as time passes. They also may be dependent on whether they are seen from the agency's or group's perspective.

Shifts in services and problems may result from previous services and problems. Changes may be influenced by community perceptions and needs. They can mirror changes within agencies or groups. Finally, changes in services and problems may indicate differing views of agencies and groups toward each other.

Ideally, agency services to groups should be reductionistic in nature. By encouraging groups to become autonomous and self-sufficient, services should make themselves redundant. However, groups may become dependent on agency services and press for more. Services also may be serial; as the need for some decreases, the need for others may develop.

Problems between self-help groups and family service agencies should be ventilated and resolved. Communication between the two types of organizations should be such that new problems do not arise. However, like services, problems may build upon each other or occur in succession.

Self-help groups and family service agencies both exist within larger communities. What these communities think of them influence the group-agency relationship. A self-help group stressing advocacy may engender public reaction which limits its relationship to a community-sensitive family service agency. Self-help groups may not want extensive relations with an agency held in low regard in its community. Communities have needs; how these needs are perceived and changes in perception by agencies and groups may affect whether and how the two types of organizations relate.

The self-help group--family service agency relationship may be altered by changes in the agencies' resources, staff, leadership, and clientele. It can be modified by changes in the self-help group's leaders, membership, and resources.

Finally, the reality of a family service agency, self-help group, or their relationship may not be as important as the perception of that reality. A group's view of an agency may be limited to the professional that works with it. An agency may know little about a group's activities but relate to it because it covers a certain problem area.

To analyze changes in the relationships of self-help groups and family service agencies and the reason for these changes necessitates a longitudinal study, perhaps a year or two in length, with measures of agency-group relations at regular and uniform points. Family service agencies of different sizes, auspices, and clientele, and with various amounts of experience and present relationships with self-help groups, would be utilized. Ideally, their relationships with groups would differ by problem, auspices, goals, and clientele. Agency group relationships would be studied from their inception. Both family service agencies and self-help groups would be surveyed as to changes in services, problems, and other aspects of relation-ships. The variety of contributing factors pre-viously mentioned would be explored.

The structure and operational format for this in-depth study of the interaction of self-help groups and family service agencies over time would be developed by Family Service America with input from participating member agencies and representa-tives of self-help groups.

Reasons for Optimism

These recommendations are made in an atmosphere of realistic optimism. Mutually beneficial rela-tionships exist between family service agencies and self-help groups. One goal of this study is to show ways in which these relationships can be made even more beneficial to agencies, groups, and society at large.

FSA SELF-HELP STUDY
Section I: Agency Form

1. Agency Name _____

2. Person FSA can contact about work with self-help
   groups _____

3. Agency's general services about self-help
   groups:

   o Does agency provide information about self-
     help groups in the community? ___Yes ___No

   o Does agency make referrals to self-help
     groups? ___Yes ___No
     Please enclose any related referral policies,
     if available.

   o Does agency encourage self-help groups to
     connect with each other? ___Yes ___No
     If yes:
         To exchange services?
         ___Yes ___No
         To join forces for advocacy?
         ___Yes ___No
         To exchange information?
         ___ Yes ___No
         Other? Please explain: _____

o   Does agency offer services to representatives
    of several self-help groups in common?
    (Arrangements with individual groups are
    reported in Section II, the Self-Help Group
    Form.) ___Yes ___No   If yes, do such
    services include:
        Leadership training?
        ___ Yes ___No
        Training to organize or administer groups?
        ___ Yes ___No
        Information on community or agency re-
        sources?
        ___ Yes ___No
        Information about personal relationships?
        ___ Yes ___No
        Other services? Please describe: _____

4. Assessment

o   Has agency work with self-help groups been
    (check one): Increasing? ___ Decreasing? ___
    Remaining the same? ___   Agency does not work
    with self-help groups ___

o   Does agency policy limit activity with self-
    help groups generally? If so, please explain:
    _____

o   Does agency wish to expand its work with
    self-help groups? ___Yes ___No If yes
    (underline one):
    We (would) (would not) be interested in par-
    ticipating in a one-year cooperative activity
    with FSA:
    ___ If paid for it. ___ Whether paid or not.

o   We (would) (would not) be willing actively to
    recruit new agreements with self-help groups:
        ___ With direct FSA guidance only.
        ___ Whether or not FSA provides guidance.
        ___ But would not wish to work with FSA.

5. Do you agree with this statement?   (Check response closest to your own.)

"FSA SHOULD INFORM AND HELP AGENCIES IN THEIR WORK WITH SELF-HELP GROUPS."

___ Agree. FSA should develop this into a modality with accompanying standards, as it has for counseling, family life education/development/enrichment, and family advocacy.

___ Agree. We expect increasing activity in this area.

___ Agree. There are problems and pitfalls in working with self-help groups that need to be better understood.

___ Neutral. No opinion, don't know.

___ Disagree. It will take away from other, more important priorities at FSA.

___ Disagree. Working with self-help groups doesn't call for national attention.

___ Disagree. Self-help groups are not in the realm of a family service agency.

FSA SELF-HELP STUDY
Section II: Self-Help Group Form

6. Agency Name _____

7. Identifying information about Self-Help Group*

   o Name of Group _____

   o Is the group a part of a larger network?
      ___Yes ___No   If yes, is it:
      ___ Local only? ___ Statewide? ___National?

   o Approximate number participating in group ___

   o In your opinion, the group's basic mission
      is: _____

8. Self-Help Group Participants

   o Does this group mostly serve:
      A particular ethnic group? ___Yes ___No   If
      yes, please identify: _____
      A particular income level? ___Yes ___No   If
      yes:
      ___ Low income? ___ Middle income? ___ High
      income?

   o Does the group particularly concern itself
      with:
      ___ Aged persons?
      ___ Developmentally disabled persons?
      ___ Child abuse or neglect?
      ___ Foster care or institutional care?

---

*For purposes of this study, self-help groups are
defined as PRIMARY GROUPS WHICH ARE DIRECTED TO
PERSONAL OR SOCIAL CONCERNS, AND WHICH DEPEND
PRIMARILY ON THEIR OWN MEMBERS' PARTICIPATION TO
CONTROL AND IMPLEMENT THEIR PROGRAMS.

9. Group Objectives. Does this group focus on:

___ Individual members' problems? If so, please try to provide a general statement about their nature: _____

___ Self-improvement (rather than specific problems)? If possible, please describe: _____

___ Supporting a way of life, or philosophy? If possible, please describe the aim: _____

___ Intervening to change social conditions? If checked, please indicate how participants perceive these conditions, whether they themselves are particularly affected, or whether these are conditions which are universal or experienced by others.
   ___ Participants particularly experience them.
   ___ All people, or others, experience them.
These conditions are (please describe): ____

___ None of the above. Please describe objectives: _____

10. Your Agency's Activity with the Group

This group is organized:
___ Under agency auspices.
___ Through the auspices of another group.
___ Independently, by its participants alone.

Your staff provides this group with:
___ Its primary leadership.
___ Professional consultation in carrying out the basic program of the group as a whole.
___ Professional back-up to help with personal problems identified within the group.
___ Training or education.
___ Financing, or help to find funds.

____ Administrative and/or physical support (as
meeting space, clerical service, photo-
copying, bookkeeping, etc.).
____ Connecting and/or informing the group about
community resources beyond those in the
agency.
____ Organizing and/or recruiting activities.
____ Referrals of potential participants.
____ Research and/or information development to
help group carry out its own objectives.
____ Other. Please describe: _____

Please check problems you may have encountered
working with this group:

____ Problems with auspices, control (for exam-
ple, over who "owns" the group).
____ Difficulty recruiting for the group.
____ Financing.
   ____ For your work with the group.
   ____ For financing for the group.
____ Competition between the group and the agen-
cy's service program.
____ Overdependence on the agency.
____ Too much or too little activity demanded of
participants in group.
____ Group activity inappropriate for most par-
ticipants. Comments: _____
____ Differences between agency and group over
ethics and/or ideology.
____ Inadequate group leadership.
____ Lack of coordination between agency and
group.
____ Problems with the nature of participation by
group members. Comments: _____
____ Difficulties with cohesion within the group.
____ Keeping the group alive.
____ Community institutions hostile to this
group's activities.
____ Others. Please describe: _____

11. Status of Cooperation

    ___ Group is continuing to work cooperatively
         with agency.
    ___ Cooperative work has been discontinued.
        ___ By agency.
        ___ By group.
        ___ By mutual agreement.
        ___ No specific cause.
        ___ Group no longer functioning.

BIBLIOGRAPHY

Biegel, David E., and Naparstek, Arthur J. (Eds.)
Community Support Systems and Mental Health: Prac-
tice, Policy, and Research. New York: Springer
Publishing Co., 1982.

Borkman, Thomasina, "Experimental Knowledge: A New
Concept for the Analysis of Self-Help Groups,"
Social Service Review 1976, 50, pp 445-456.

Borman, Leonard, "Action Anthropology and the Self-
Help/Mutual Aid Movement," Hinshaw, R. (Ed.) in
Currents in Anthropology: Essays in Honor of Sol
Tax. The Hague: Mouton, 1979, pp 487-511.

Chutis, Laurieann, Self-Help Mutual Aid Groups and
Community Mental Health Centers - Effective Partners. New York, City University of New York, National Self-Help Clearinghouse, 1980.

Coplon, Jennifer, and Strull, Judith, "Role of the
Professional in Mutual Aid Groups," Social Casework, 1983, 64, 5, pp 259-266.

Dumont, Matthew P., "Self-Help Treatment Programs:
An Overview," American Journal of Psychiatry, 1974,
131, pp 631-635.

Durman, Eugene L., "The Role of Self Help Groups in Service Provision," Journal of Applied Behavioral Science, 1976, 12, pp 433-443.

Family Service Association of America, New Opportunities for Services to Families (Wingspread Conference). New York: Family Service Association of America, 1981.

Froland, Charles, "Community Support Systems: All Things to All People?" Biegel, David E. and Naparstek, Arthur J. (Eds.) in Community Support Systems and Mental Health: Practice, Policy and Research. New York: Springer Publishing Co., 1982, pp 253-266.

Garland, James A.; Jones, Hubert E.; and Kolodny, Ralph L., "A Model for Stages of Development in Social Work Groups," Bernstein, Saul (Ed.) in Explorations in Group Work: Essays in Theory and Practice. Charlestown, Mass.: Charles River Books, 1976, pp 17-71.

Gartner, Allen, and Riessman, Frank, Self-help in the Human Services. San Francisco: Jossey-Bass, 1977.

Gottlieb, Benjamin H., "Lay Influences on the Utilization and Provision of Health Services," Canadian Psychological Review, 1976, 17, pp 126-136.

Gussow, A., and Tracy, G., "The Role of Self-Help Clubs in Adaptation to Chronic Illness and Disability." Social Science and Medicine, 1976, 10, pp 407-414.

Heiman, Mark A., Mantell, Joanne E., and Alexander, Esther S., "Collaboration and Its Discontents: The Perils of Partnership," Journal of Applied Behavioral Science, 1976, 12, pp 403-410.

Hurvitz, Nathan, "The Origins of the Peer Self-Help Psychotherapy Group Movement," Journal of Applied Behavioral Science, 1976, 12, 3, pp 283-295.

Initiatives for Community Self-Help: Efforts to Increase Recognition and Support. New York: The New World Foundation, 1980.

Katz, Alfred H., and Bender, E., "Self-Help Groups in Western Society: History and Prospects," Journal of Applied Behavioral Science, 1976, 12, 3, pp 265-282.

Katz, Alfred H., and Bender, E., The Strength in Us: Self-Help Groups in the Modern World. New York: New Viewpoints, 1976.

Larson, J.; Norris, E.; and Kroll, J., Consultation and Its Outcome: Community Mental Health Centers. Palo Alto, Cal., American Institute for Research, 1976.

Levy, Leon, "Self Help Groups: Types and Psychological Processes," Journal of Applied Behavioral Science, 1976, 12, 3, pp 310-322.

Lieberman, Morton A., and Borman, Leonard (Eds.) Self-Help Groups for Coping with Crisis. San Francisco: Jossey-Bass, 1979.

Maguire, Lambart, "Natural Helping Networks and Self-Help Groups," Noble, M. (Ed.) in Primary Prevention in Mental Health and Social Work. New York: Council on Social Work Education, 1981.

Milofsky, Carl, Structure and Process in Self-Help Organizations. New Haven: Yale University, Institution for Social and Policy Studies, 1980.

President's Commission on Mental Health. Task Panel Reports (Vol. II-IV). Washington, D.C.: U.S. Government Printing Office, 1978.

Riessman, Frank, "Self-Help and the Professional," keynote address, Conference on the Self-Help Movement and Human Service Professionals: New Ways of Working Together, Long Island Self-Help Clearinghouse, New York Institute of Technology. Old Westbury, N.Y., Jan. 18, 1979.

Shaw, Robert, The Role of United Way Agencies with Self Help Groups. St. Louis: Family and Children's Service of Greater St. Louis, 1983.

Silverman, Phyllis R., et al. (Eds.) Helping Each Other in Widowhood. New York: Health Sciences, 1974.

Silverman, Phyllis R., "The Mental Health Consultant as a Linking Agent," Biegel, David E., and Naparstek, Arthur J. (Eds.) in Community Support Systems and Mental Health: Practice, Policy, and Research. New York: Springer Publishing Co., 1982, pp 238-249.

Silverman, Phyllis, Mutual Help Groups: A Guide for Mental Health Workers. Bethesda, Md.: National Institute of Mental Health, 1978.

Spiegel, David, "Self-help and Mutual-support Groups: A Synthesis of the Recent Literature." Biegel, D., and Naparstek, A. (Eds.) in Community Support Systems and Mental Health: Practice, Policy, and Research. New York: Springer Publishing Co., 1982, pp 98-117.

Steinman, Richard, and Traunstein, Donald M., "Redefining Deviance: The Self-Help Challenge to the Human Services," Journal of Applied Behavioral Science, 1976, 12, pp 347-361.

Todres, Rubin,"Professional Attitudes Towards Self-Help Groups," Self-Help Reporter, 12/81, p 6.

Vallance, Theodore R., and D'Angelli, Anthony R., "The Professional as a Developer of Natural Helping Systems: Conceptual, Organizational, and Pragmatic Considerations," Biegel, D., and Naparstek, A. (Eds.) in Community Support Systems and Mental Health: Practice, Policy, and Research. New York: Springer Publishing Co., 1982, pp 224-237.

The White House Conference on Families, Listening to America's Families Action for the 80's. Washington, D.C., The White House Conference on Families, 1980.